T0049464

THE BRITISH ARE COMING

RICK ATKINSON

WITH KATE WATERS

Adapted from *The British Are Coming*

Godwin Books
Henry Holt and Company
New York

Based on the book *The British Are Coming* by Rick Atkinson

Henry Holt and Company, *Publishers since 1866*
Henry Holt® is a registered trademark of Macmillan Publishing Group, LLC
120 Broadway, New York, NY 10271 • mackids.com

Library of Congress Cataloging-in-Publication Data

Our books may be purchased in bulk for promotional, educational, or business use. Please contact your local bookseller or the Macmillan Corporate and Premium Sales Department at (800) 221-7945 ext. 5442 or by email at MacmillanSpecialMarkets@macmillan.com.

Names: Atkinson, Rick, author. | Waters, Kate. | Atkinson, Rick. British are coming.
Title: The British are coming / Rick Atkinson ; with Kate Waters.
Description: First edition. | New York : Godwin Books, Henry Holt and Company, 2022. |
"Adapted from The British Are Coming." | Includes bibliographical references and index. |
Audience: Ages 8-12 | Audience: Grades 4-6 | Summary: "A young readers edition
of Rick Atkinson's The British Are Coming"—Provided by publisher.
Identifiers: LCCN 2021049886 | ISBN 9781250800589 (hardcover)
Subjects: LCSH: United States—History—Revolution, 1775-1783—Campaigns.
Classification: LCC E230 .A845 2022 | DDC 973.3—dc23/eng/20211207
LC record available at https://lccn.loc.gov/2021049886

First edition, 2022 / Designed by Sarah Nichole Kaufman
Maps by Gene Thorp
Printed in the United States of America by BVG–Fairfield, Fairfield, Pennsylvania

1 3 5 7 9 10 8 6 4 2

I am now Imbarkd on a tempestuous Ocean
from whence, perhaps, no friendly harbour is to be found.

GEORGE WASHINGTON
TO BURWELL BASSETT, JUNE 19, 1775

MAP LEGEND

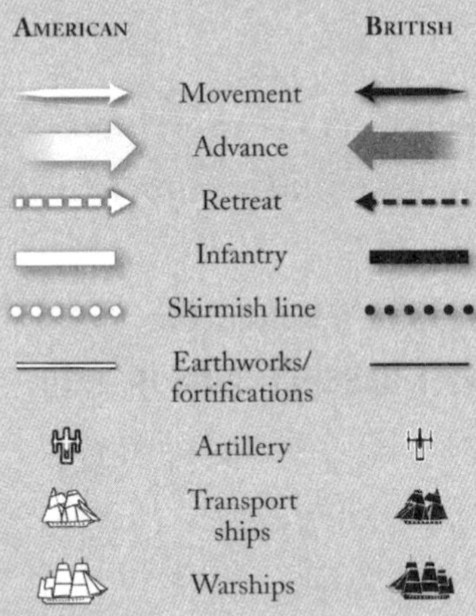

FEATURES

City/Town
Capital
House
Tavern
Church
Hall/Meeting house/
Prison/Theater/
College
Mill
Fort
Cemetery
Bridge
Pass
Other feature
Clash
Previous engagement
Burned

Road
River
Boundary
Fence
Rail fence
Stone wall
Body of water
Woods
Marsh
Mudflat
Beach
Terrain
Highlighted terrain

A Union Jack appears on some maps to signify British positions; no comparable American national flag was yet in wide use early in the war.

Boundaries and geographic labels generally reflect British cartographic surveys from the mid-eighteenth-century. Borders often were disputed.

TABLE OF CONTENTS

PARTIAL TIMELINE OF THE AMERICAN REVOLUTION

1773 – 1777

1773

MAY 10 The Tea Act, passed by Parliament, takes effect.

DECEMBER 16 Patriots protest the Tea Act by throwing bales of tea from British ships into Boston Harbor.

1774

MARCH Parliament passes the first of the Coercive Acts to punish Boston for the Tea Party.

MAY British General Thomas Gage become new royal governor of Massachusetts.

SEPTEMBER The first Continental Congress meets in Philadelphia to discuss the tense situation with Great Britain.

OCTOBER Massachusetts begins to make preparations for war.

1775

JANUARY 20 Both houses of Parliament petition King George III to declare Massachusetts in rebellion and to take all measures needed to bring American rebels to heel.

MARCH 23 Patrick Henry delivers his famous "Give me liberty, or give me death" speech at the Virginia legislature.

MARCH Virginia governor declares martial law in the state.

APRIL 14 Massachusetts governor Thomas Gage is told to put down open rebellion of the colonists using all force necessary.

APRIL 18 Paul Revere and William Dawes, Jr., set out on horseback for Concord and Lexington in Massachusetts to warn patriot leaders that British soldiers are marching from Boston.

APRIL 19 The first shots are fired between minutemen and British soldiers.

APRIL 19 The British retreat to Boston.

MAY Second Continental Congress meets in Philadelphia and appoints John Hancock as its president.

JUNE 12 General Thomas Gage declares martial law in Boston.

JUNE 17 American militiamen are forced to retreat after the battle of Bunker Hill, but the British suffer heavy casualties.

JUNE 19 George Washington is appointed commander in chief of the new Continental Army.

JULY 3 Washington takes command of the army outside Boston.

DECEMBER 31 The Continental Army under General Richard Montgomery and Colonel Benedict Arnold is defeated in an attempt to capture Quebec, Canada.

DECEMBER King George declares the American colonies closed to trade as of March 1776.

1776

JANUARY 10 Thomas Paine's "Common Sense" is published.

MARCH 17 British general William Howe abandons Boston, sailing to Halifax, Nova Scotia. The patriots reclaim Boston.

JULY 4 Congress adopts the Declaration of Independence.

JULY A massive British force arrives at New York by sea, landing first on Staten Island before shifting to Long Island.

AUGUST 27 Howe defeats George Washington at the Battle of Long Island and soon recaptures New York City.

SEPTEMBER 22 Nathan Hale is executed by the British for spying.

DECEMBER Pushed out of New York and New Jersey, Washington and his army retreat into Pennsylvania. Congress flees from Philadelphia to Baltimore.

DECEMBER 21 Benjamin Franklin arrives in Paris as the senior American diplomat in France.

DECEMBER 25 Washington crosses the Delaware River on Christmas night and routs the Hessian garrison in Trenton, New Jersey.

1777

JANUARY 3 Washington's army defeats a British detachment at Princeton, New Jersey.

KEY PLAYERS

ADAMS, ABIGAIL: wife of John Adams

ADAMS, JOHN: Boston lawyer who became an American statesman and served in France during the Revolutionary War

ADAMS, SAMUEL: American political leader; considered a Founding Father of the United States

ARANDA, COUNT DE: Spanish ambassador to France

ARNOLD, BENEDICT: colonel who led the American invasion of Canada

BURGOYNE, JOHN: British general in Quebec

CADWALADER, JOHN: American colonel in charge of Pennsylvania troops at Valley Forge

CARLETON, GUY: British governor of Quebec and commander of troops

CARON, PIERRE-AUGUSTIN: known as Beaumarchais; a French merchant tasked with sending money to Americans

CLINTON, HENRY: British general and commander in chief

CORNWALLIS, CHARLES: British general

DAWES, WILLIAM, Jr.: horse messenger among rebel cities

FRANKLIN, BENJAMIN: American diplomat and member of the Continental Congress

FRASER, MALCOLM: British captain in Quebec

GAGE, THOMAS: British commander in chief in the American colonies early in the war

GEORGE III: king of England

GERMAIN, GEORGE, LORD: King George's secretary of state for the American department

GLOVER, JOHN: Massachusetts colonel commanding the American 14th Continental Regiment

GRAVES, SAMUEL: British commander of the North American Station

GREENE, NATHANAEL: commander of American defenses on Long Island

HALE, NATHAN: American captain who volunteered to be a spy behind British lines on Long Island

HANCOCK, JOHN: prominent American rebel leader and the first person to sign the Declaration of Independence

HARCOURT, WILLIAM: British colonel in charge of the 16th Light Dragoons, who captured Charles Lee

HITCHCOCK, DANIEL: American colonel with the New England brigade

HOWE, RICHARD, LORD: admiral and commander of the British armada

HOWE, WILLIAM: British senior major general in Boston, then commander in chief of British troops

KNOWLTON, THOMAS: American leader of the Rangers

KNOX, HENRY: American soldier who moved cannon from Ticonderoga and served as advisor to Washington

KNYPHAUSEN, WILHELM VON: Hessian general

LEE, CHARLES: American general, second in command to Washington, in charge of the southern forces

LOUIS XVI: king of France

MAGAW, ROBERT: American colonel commanding Fort Washington, New York

MAWHOOD, CHARLES: British lieutenant colonel who led the unsuccessful defense of Princeton

MERCER, HUGH: American general who died defending Princeton

MONTGOMERY, RICHARD: American brigadier general who led the unsuccessful invasion of Quebec

MOULTRIE, WILLIAM: American commander of Fort Sullivan

MOWAT, HENRY: lieutenant and British flotilla commander

NORTH, FREDERICK: childhood friend and advisor to King George

PARKER, JOHN: captain of the American militiamen at Concord

PARKER, PETER: commodore and naval commander of British troops off Charleston, South Carolina

PERCY, HUGH, EARL: British brigadier who led reinforcements at Concord

PIGOT, ROBERT: British brigadier general and commander of the left flank of General Howe's army at Bunker Hill

PITCAIRN, JOHN: British marine commander in Boston and a leader in the battles of Lexington and Concord; later killed at Bunker Hill

PRESCOTT, WILLIAM: American colonel at Bunker Hill

PRESTON, CHARLES: British commander of Fort St. Johns in Canada

PUTNAM, ISRAEL: American general commanding troops in Boston

RALL, JOHANN GOTTLIEB: German colonel in charge of grenadiers in Trenton

REED, JOSEPH: American colonel and advisor to Washington

REVERE, PAUL: Boston silversmith who carried dispatches to military and civilian rebels

SCHUYLER, PHILIP: major general of the Northern Army, and later an advisor to Washington

STARK, JOHN: American colonel and commander of New Hampshire militiamen at Bunker Hill

ST. CLAIR, ARTHUR: general whose brigade held the American right wing at the Battle of Trenton

STIRLING, WILLIAM ALEXANDER: American general who held off British forces on Long Island long enough for Washington to evacuate

SULLIVAN, JOHN: commander of American forces in Quebec after John Thomas died of smallpox

THOMAS, JOHN: briefly commander of American forces in Quebec; died of smallpox during the retreat

THOMSON, WILLIAM: American colonel defending Sullivan's Island

TRYON, WILLIAM: British governor of New York

WARREN, JOSEPH: prominent Boston physician and orator

WASHINGTON, GEORGE: American general and commander in chief

WASHINGTON, MARTHA: wife of George Washington

WOOSTER, DAVID: general and Continental commander of the rear guard in Montreal

AUTHOR'S NOTE

My ancestors who came to America from England in the late 1600s were Quaker pacifists whose religion prohibited support of any war. As far as I can tell, their descendants in the 1770s took no active role in the American Revolution, either as rebel patriots fighting for independence or loyalists struggling to keep their allegiance to King George III and the British empire. In that regard, they were like many people among the 2.5 million Americans in 1776—and not just Quakers—who tried to remain neutral and avoid the awful dangers that war brought.

Despite not having a personal connection to those turbulent events, I've been fascinated by the Revolution since I was a kid. As an eighth grader in Kansas, I wrote a report on General Benedict Arnold, trying to understand why the finest soldier in the American cause would betray his country and join the British Army. The dramatic stories of Lexington and Concord, where the war began, fired my imagination, along with the battle of Bunker Hill, General George Washington's surprise attack across the Delaware River on Christmas night in 1776, the suffering at Valley Forge, and many other episodes in a struggle that lasted for eight years. Those events *still* have a grip on my imagination.

Whether your family came to America three centuries ago or last year, the story of the Revolution tells us who we are and where we came from as a nation, what our forebears believed, and what they were willing to fight for. It's an exciting tale of courage, doubt, sacrifice, and bitter disagreement. I hope that you'll find it as fascinating as I did as a young reader, because those events of long ago still shape the world you live in today.

Rick Atkinson

Washington, D.C.

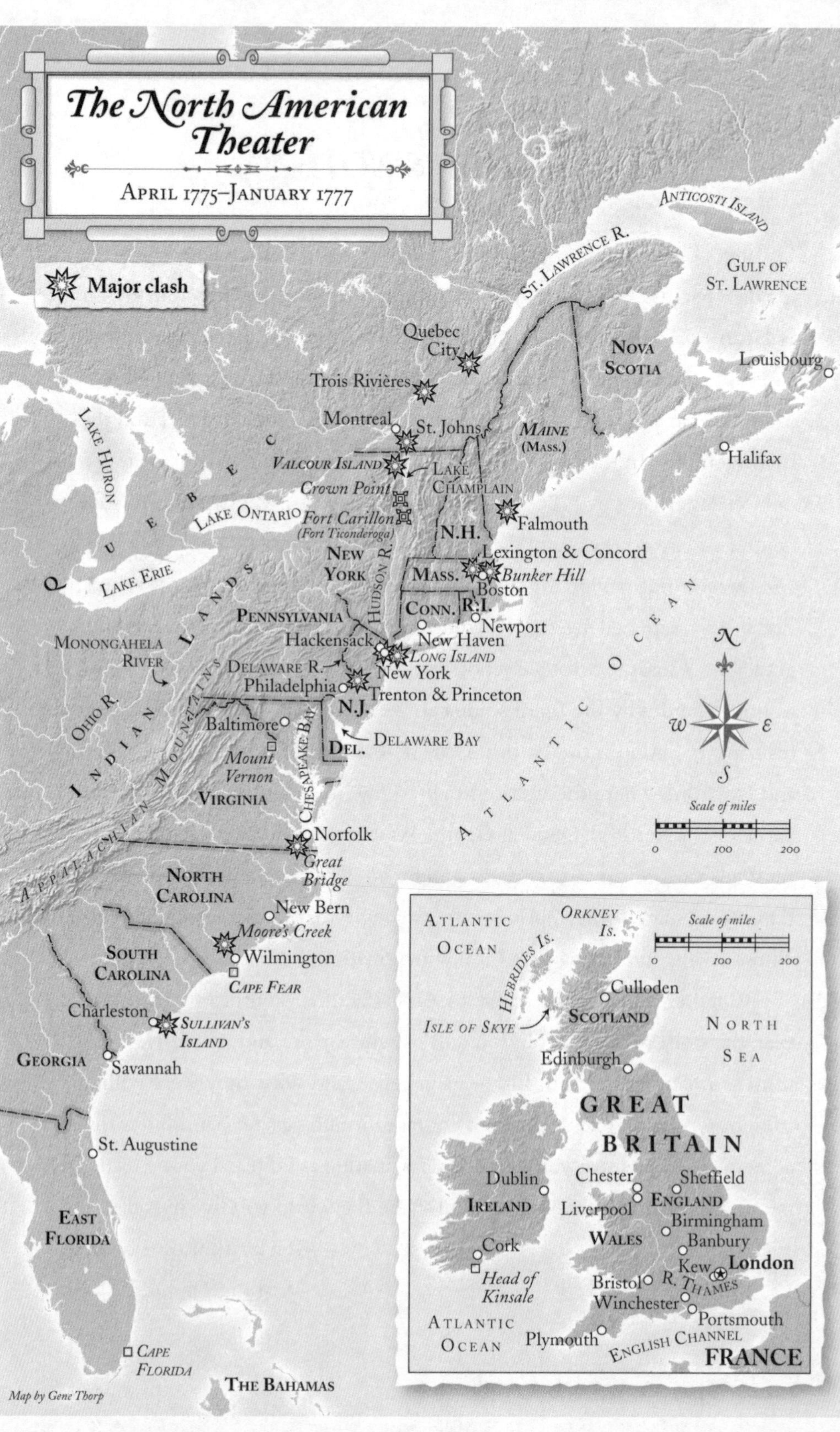

The North American Theater
April 1775–January 1777
Major clash
Anticosti Island
St. Lawrence R.
Gulf of St. Lawrence
Quebec City
Nova Scotia
Louisbourg
Trois Rivières
Montreal
St. Johns
Maine (Mass.)
Halifax
Lake Huron
Quebec
Valcour Island
Lake Champlain
Crown Point
Lake Ontario
Fort Carillon (Fort Ticonderoga)
Falmouth
N.H.
New York
Hudson R.
Lexington & Concord
Mass.
Bunker Hill
Boston
Lake Erie
Indian Lands
Pennsylvania
Conn.
R.I.
Newport
New Haven
Monongahela River
Hackensack
Long Island
Delaware R.
New York
Atlantic Ocean
Philadelphia
Trenton & Princeton
Ohio R.
N.J.
Baltimore
Chesapeake Bay
Delaware Bay
W
E
N
S
Del.
Mount Vernon
Appalachian Mountains
Virginia
Scale of miles
0
100
200
Norfolk
Great Bridge
North Carolina
New Bern
Moore's Creek
Wilmington
South Carolina
Cape Fear
Charleston
Sullivan's Island
Georgia
Savannah
St. Augustine
East Florida
Cape Florida
The Bahamas
Map by Gene Thorp
Atlantic Ocean
Orkney Is.
Hebrides Is.
Scale of miles
0
100
200
Culloden
Scotland
Isle of Skye
North Sea
Edinburgh
Great Britain
Dublin
Chester
Sheffield
Ireland
Liverpool
England
Birmingham
Wales
Banbury
Cork
Kew
London
Head of Kinsale
Bristol
R. Thames
Winchester
Portsmouth
Atlantic Ocean
Plymouth
English Channel
France

ONE

THE COURT OF KING GEORGE III

1773–1775

On the evening of December 16, 1773, a few dozen American colonists, men with their faces darkened by lampblack or charcoal, descended with war whoops down Milk Street in Boston to board three merchant ships moored at Griffin's Wharf. Prying open the hatches, they used pulleys to lift from the holds hundreds of heavy chests containing forty-five tons of tea. For three hours they smashed the lids and scooped the tea leaves into the harbor.

BOSTON TEA PARTY, DECEMBER 16, 1773. [LOC]

Accomplices in small boats used rakes and oars to scatter the floating piles, and by morning almost £10,000 worth of soggy brown flakes drifted from the wharf to Castle Island and the Dorchester shore. "The devil is in these people," a British naval officer wrote after seeing the damage. But a local lawyer exulted. "This destruction of the tea," John Adams declared, "is so bold, so daring, so firm, intrepid, & inflexible." A silversmith named Paul Revere carried a detailed account of the event to New York and Philadelphia in the first of his famous gallops.

"I am much hurt," King George III confessed in mid-January 1774 when news of this outrage reached him in London. As king of Great Britain since 1760, his realm also included the thirteen American colonies. Sorrow soon yielded to anger. What should be done? Confusion and uncertainty plagued the government, which was beset with conflicting reports and opinions. Was this challenge to British authority widespread or limited to a few scoundrels in New England? Was reconciliation possible?

Friction between the colonies and the mother country had been building for almost a decade. Colonists resented being taxed by Britain without representation in Parliament, Britain's lawmaking body in London. In England, many thought of the colonists as spoiled, ungrateful children.

KING GEORGE III. [LOC]

However, some London merchants signed petitions urging caution, for fear that the loss of American markets would cripple their businesses. The colonists bought up to 20 percent of British manufactured goods, but the market for certain commodities was much bigger—a quarter of British salt; a third of sugar, tin, and wool socks; half of copper utensils, glassware, and silk goods; and two thirds to three quarters of iron nails, boat ropes, and beaver hats.

The king's heart hardened. Rejecting petitions and appeals from those pleading for moderation, he vowed in March 1774 to "stop the present disorders." To British lawmakers in Parliament, which included the House of Commons and the House of Lords, he denounced "a dangerous spirit of resistance" in America among "my deluded subjects."

The king and his advisors believed that British wealth and status derived from its colonies. The erosion of authority in America would encourage rebellions in the other colonies of Canada, Ireland, the Caribbean, and India. With the empire broken up, an impoverished Great Britain, no longer great, would invite "the scorn of Europe" and exploitation by enemies in France, Spain, and elsewhere. Those piles of wet tea leaves foretold political and economic ruin.

A VIEW OF BOSTON FROM THE HARBOR. *[LOC]*

From late March through June 1774, Parliament adopted laws known collectively in Britain as the Coercive Acts (and later in America as the Intolerable Acts). The first was punitive: Boston's port must close until the cost of the ruined tea was paid to the East India Company, which traded goods, including the destroyed tea, with the colonies. The other laws tightened British control over Massachusetts. British troops would occupy Boston under a commander in chief who would also serve as the royal governor. In a separate session, Parliament approved expanding the boundaries of its Canadian territory to the west and south, to the rich territory between the Mississippi and Ohio Rivers. Infuriated American colonists felt that they were being confined to the Atlantic coast.

"The die is now cast," King George wrote. "The colonies must either submit or triumph. We must not retreat."

TWO

ST. STEPHEN'S CHAPEL, PALACE OF WESTMINSTER, LONDON

January 1775

On January 19, 1775, the House of Commons reconvened in St. Stephen's Chapel after the Christmas holiday. With a thud, a clerk dropped 149 documents on a central table, announced that they were "papers relating to the disturbances in North America," and in a somber tone began to read the titles of each: Royal Navy dispatches from American waters; seditious extracts from the Continental Congress; reports written by royal officials from New Hampshire to Georgia; official correspondence from London to colonial governors.

Slouched on a bench was Lord Frederick North, a childhood friend of King George. He supervised the national finances as head of the Treasury Board. Steadfastly loyal to the king and skilled in debate, North was the principal defender of government policy in the Commons. In the past year he had delivered more than one hundred speeches relating to the American colony, most of them harsh.

Now he was fated to be a war minister, with his king's empire in the balance. He could talk tough, as in his claim that "America must fear you before they will love you" or his assurance to the Commons that "four or five frigates" could close Boston Harbor because "the militia of Boston [are] no match for the force of this country."

LORD FREDERICK NORTH. [LOC]

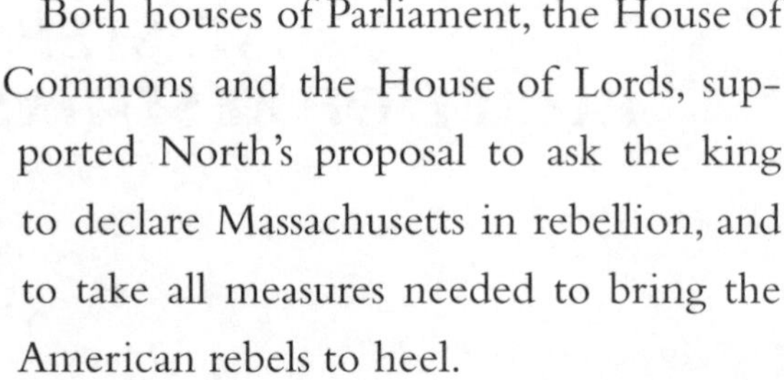

Both houses of Parliament, the House of Commons and the House of Lords, supported North's proposal to ask the king to declare Massachusetts in rebellion, and to take all measures needed to bring the American rebels to heel.

The next day hundreds of members of both houses paraded to St. James's Palace for the king to hear their petition:

> *We find that a part of your Majesty's subjects in the province of the [Massachusetts] Bay have proceeded so far to resist the authority of the supreme legislature, that a rebellion at this time actually exists . . . We consider it as our indispensable duty, humbly to beseech your Majesty that you will take the most effectual measures to enforce due obedience to the laws and authority of the supreme legislature.*

King George replied:

> *You may depend on my taking the most speedy and effectual measures for enforcing due obedience to the laws . . . It is my ardent wish that this disposition may have a happy effect on the temper and conduct of my subjects in America.*

Events now moved swiftly. That very day the king ordered several regiments in Ireland to prepare for "foreign service."

And so war stuffs were gathered to be loaded onto westbound ships: canteens, leather cartridge boxes, overcoats, tents, five-ton wagons by the dozen, muskets by the hundreds, powder by the ton. And there was a run on New World maps.

Troops tramped toward the ports. Each regiment was also permitted to take sixty women, twelve servants, and eighty-six tons of baggage.

No one could foresee that the American War of Independence would last 3,059 days. Or that the struggle would be marked by more than 1,300 actions, mostly small and bloody, with a few large and bloody, plus 241 naval engagements in a theater initially bounded by the Atlantic seaboard, the St. Lawrence and Mississippi Rivers, and the Gulf of Mexico.

The odds were heavily stacked against the Americans: No colonial rebellion had ever succeeded in casting off imperial shackles.

THREE

BOSTON, MASSACHUSETTS

March 6, 1775

In the nine months since British warships had closed the port, warehouses stood vacant, shipyards idle, wharves deserted, shop shelves empty. Only a bountiful local crop of lambs and charity from other colonies kept Bostonians from hunger: fish and flour from elsewhere in New England, rice from the Carolinas, rye from Baltimore, a thousand bushels of wheat from Quebec, cash from Delaware and Montreal.

Town selectmen launched projects to employ the unemployed—street paving, well digging, building a new brickyard. But gangs of idle sailors, longshoremen, rope makers, riggers, and carpenters could often be found loitering by the docks or in the town's ninety taverns.

On Monday morning, March 6, the "gloomy place" abruptly sprang to life. Hundreds and then thousands filled the streets to commemorate the bloody 1770 brawl between an unruly mob and British soldiers that had left five civilians dead in what was now known as the Boston Massacre.

THE BOSTON MASSACRE OF 1770. *[NYPL]*

Dr. Joseph Warren, a prominent local physician, intended to deliver a speech titled "The Baleful Influence of Standing Armies in Time of Peace" in the Old South Meeting House. An uneasy murmur rose from the congregants. It was rumored that mass arrests were likely this morning, and that British officers had agreed that if the king was insulted, they would draw swords and slaughter the offenders. The murmur in Old South grew louder when several dozen red-coated officers clumped through the doorway and stood in the aisles.

THE OLD SOUTH CHURCH, BOSTON. *[LOC]*

Rising to the pulpit, Dr. Warren invoked the long struggle to carve a country from the New England wilderness. He described Britain's recent efforts to assert authority over the country, and the shootings five years before that had left "the stones bespattered with your father's brains." Then came the Coercive Acts, insult upon injury. "Our wish is that Britain and the colonies may, like the oak and the ivy, grow and increase in strength together," Warren said. "But if these pacific measures are ineffectual, and it appears that the only way to safety is through fields of blood, I know you will not turn your faces from your foes."

Hours to the Gates of this City many Thouſands of our brave Brethren in the Country, deeply affected with our Diſtreſſes, and to whom we are greatly obliged on this Occaſion—No one knows where this would have ended, and what important Conſequences even to the whole Britiſh Empire might have followed, which our Moderation & Loyalty upon ſo trying an Occaſion, and our Faith in the Commander's Aſſurances have happily prevented.

Laſt Thurſday, agreeable to a general Requeſt of the Inhabitants, and by the Conſent of Parents and Friends, were carried to their *Graves* in Succeſſion, the Bodies of *Samuel Gray*, *Samuel Maverick*, *James Caldwell*, and *Criſpus Attucks*, the unhappy Victims who fell in the bloody Maſſacre of the Monday Evening preceeding!

On this Occaſion moſt of the Shops in Town were ſhut, all the Bells were ordered to toll a ſolemn Peal, as were alſo thoſe in the neighboring Towns of Charleſtown Roxbury, &c. The Proceſſion began to move between the Hours of 4 and 5 in the Afternoon; two of the unfortunate Sufferers, viz. Meſſ.

THE COFFINS OF FOUR MEN KILLED IN THE BOSTON MASSACRE. *[LOC]*

The six weeks following Dr. Warren's speech were filled with "dread suspense," as the Reverend William Emerson of Concord later wrote. Yet daily life plodded on. Goods smuggled or stockpiled before the port's closing could be found for a price, including candles for five shillings a pound in the Faneuil Hall market, along with blue dye and a few barrels of sugar.

American preparations for war continued. Secret military cargo had arrived all winter, smuggled from Germany, the Netherlands, even London. The Simsbury Iron Works in Connecticut cast cannonballs. Women in Salem, Massachusetts, secretly cut and stitched five thousand flannel powder cartridges for field guns. Farm carts hauled ammunition and powder kegs down country lanes, to be hidden in attics or buried in new-plowed furrows along with radish and onion seeds.

In Concord, a militia colonel listed more than three dozen

hidden stores in his notebooks—including rice, ammunition, axes, oatmeal, and wood-bladed shovels. As ordered by the provincial Committee of Supply, he appointed "faithful men" to guard the stocks, with teams ready "by day and night, on the shortest notice" to haul the supplies away as required.

In Boston, the British garrison now exceeded five thousand, of whom more than four fifths were soldiers, gunners, and marines. Ugly encounters between Bostonians and the soldiers multiplied. Bored, anxious British soldiers gambled and drank. Some deserted to the Americans.

Finally, on Friday, April 14, the orders that British commanders had expected arrived. General Thomas Gage, the British commander, opened the envelope marked secret to find his instructions:

> *It is the opinion of the King's servants, in which His Majesty concurs, that the essential step to be taken toward reestablishing government would be to arrest and imprison the principal actors and abettors in the provincial congress, whose proceedings appear in every light to be acts of treason and rebellion.*

It was agreed in London that Gage must be firm. "The king's dignity and the honor and safety of the empire require that in such a situation, force should be repelled by force," the message continued.

Gage had an undercover espionage network. Through American spies on the British payroll, he knew that militia generals had been appointed. He knew that British

LIEUTENANT GENERAL THOMAS GAGE. [LOC]

troop movements were being closely watched. Gage had been told that mounted rebel couriers could quickly rouse 7,500 minutemen—farmers and shopkeepers ready to become militia troops on a minute's notice—and that stores of military supplies were hidden in outlying settlements.

Gage had fixed on Concord, said to be the first village founded in Massachusetts Bay that was "beyond the sight and sound of the sea." Eighteen miles from Boston and now home to 265 families, it was a place where church attendance was compulsory, where the provincial congress sometimes met, and where, according to Gage's spies, munitions and other war supplies had been hidden in bulk. It was the supplies that drew his attention. He even had a hand-drawn map, crude but detailed, showing the houses, outbuildings, and other hiding places where those supplies could be found.

The Americans, too, had informants. Gage would complain that the rebels collected "good, full, and expeditious intelligence on all matters transacting in England." Reports sent from London to patriot leaders warned of regiments preparing for deployment and of the blunt new instructions sent to Gage.

Despite his orders, Gage chose not to chase suspected scoundrels across the province. That he deemed futile. Instead, he felt that a hard strike against the depot in Concord would be more fruitful, although disappointing, late intelligence indicated that the cagey rebels had evacuated at least some military stocks to other sites. But organized opposition seemed unlikely, he thought.

Gage drafted a 319-word order for Lieutenant Colonel Francis Smith of the 10th Regiment of Foot, a veteran British Army unit, to be appointed to lead the strike brigade. Smith was mature, experienced, and prudent. He was to march "with the utmost expedition and secrecy to Concord," Gage noted, adding,

> *You will seize and destroy all artillery, ammunition, provisions, tents, small arms, and all military stores whatever. But you will take care that the soldiers do not plunder the inhabitants, or hurt private property.*

The map enclosed with the order illustrated Gage's demand that two bridges over the Concord River were to be secured by an advance "party of the best marchers." Captured gunpowder and flour were to be dumped into the river, tents burned, salt pork and beef supplies destroyed. Enemy field guns should be spiked by forcing a metal rod into the firing mechanism or ruined with sledgehammers. The expedition would carry a single day's rations and no artillery; speed and surprise were essential. Sentries on horseback would be positioned to prevent rebel couriers from sounding an alarm. Gage concluded his order without sentiment: "You will open your business and return with the troops as soon as possible."

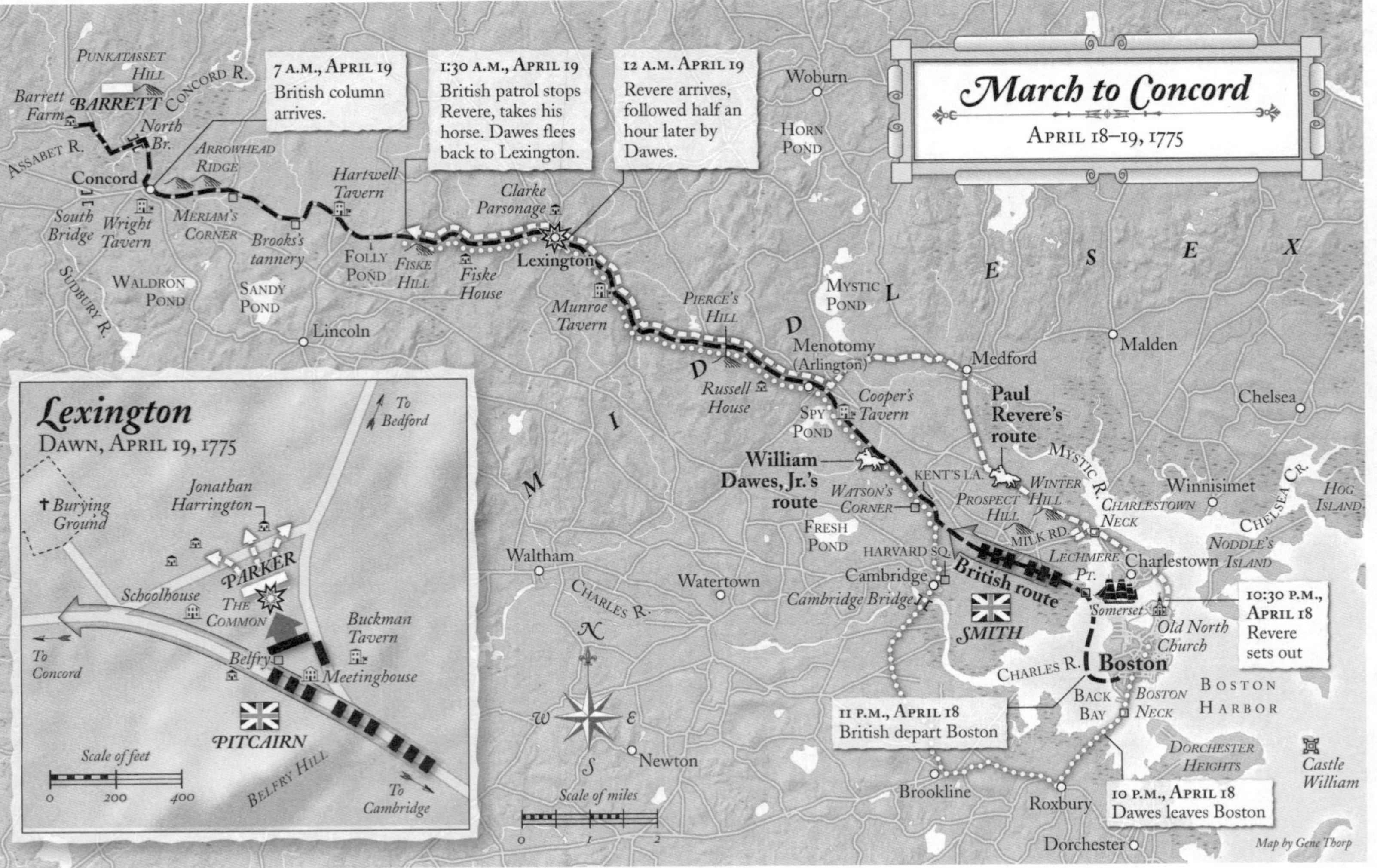

March to Concord
April 18–19, 1775
7 A.M., April 19
British column arrives.
1:30 A.M., April 19
British patrol stops Revere, takes his horse. Dawes flees back to Lexington.
12 A.M. April 19
Revere arrives, followed half an hour later by Dawes.
10:30 P.M., April 18
Revere sets out
11 P.M., April 18
British depart Boston
10 P.M., April 18
Dawes leaves Boston
Paul Revere's route
William Dawes, Jr.'s route
British route
SMITH
Punkatasset Hill
Barrett Farm
BARRETT
Concord R.
North Br.
Assabet R.
Concord
Arrowhead Ridge
South Bridge
Wright Tavern
Meriam's Corner
Brooks's tannery
Hartwell Tavern
Folly Pond
Fiske Hill
Fiske House
Clarke Parsonage
Lexington
Munroe Tavern
Sudbury R.
Waldron Pond
Sandy Pond
Lincoln
Woburn
Horn Pond
Pierce's Hill
Mystic Pond
Menotomy (Arlington)
Russell House
Spy Pond
Cooper's Tavern
Medford
Malden
Chelsea
Watson's Corner
Kent's La.
Fresh Pond
Harvard Sq.
Cambridge
Cambridge Bridge
Prospect Hill
Winter Hill
Milk Rd.
Mystic R.
Charlestown Neck
Lechmere Pt.
Charlestown
Winnisimet
Chelsea Cr.
Hog Island
Noddle's Island
Somerset
Old North Church
Boston
Charles R.
Back Bay
Boston Neck
Boston Harbor
Dorchester Heights
Castle William
Waltham
Watertown
Newton
Brookline
Roxbury
Dorchester
M I D D L E S E X
Scale of miles
0 1 2
Lexington
Dawn, April 19, 1775
To Bedford
Burying Ground
Jonathan Harrington
PARKER
Schoolhouse
The Common
Buckman Tavern
Belfry
Meetinghouse
To Concord
PITCAIRN
Belfry Hill
To Cambridge
Scale of feet
0 200 400
Map by Gene Thorp

FOUR

BOSTON, MASSACHUSETTS

April 18–19, 1775

Not until the moon rose at 10:00 p.m. on Tuesday, April 18, did shape and color emerge from the hurrying gray figures to reveal hundreds of men in blood-red coats congregating on the Boston shore. First, the eight hundred British soldiers had to be rowed to marshy Lechmere Point, a mile distant across Back Bay. Each man's kit included an eleven-pound Brown Bess musket, three dozen rounds of ammunition in a cartridge box, and a pack to carry bread and salt pork.

When the soldiers climbed from the boats and waded through the reeds on the far shore, they reached the wide, unpaved road leading west. Few knew their destination.

With their wet shoes squelching, they marched past apple and plum orchards, past smokehouses and cider mills and cow pastures. The heavy footfall rattled pewter dishes on dressers and in cupboards, and an eight-year-old boy, awake when he should have been sleeping, later recalled a wondrous sight on the road outside his window: a long bobbing column of red, "like a flowing river," sweeping northwest.

The brigade of armed men tiptoeing through Boston in the middle of the night had not gone unnoticed. Before the first boats had pulled off the Boston beach, Dr. Warren had summoned two couriers to carry the alarm to Samuel Adams and John Hancock, two prominent rebel leaders taking shelter in the nearby village of Lexington, and to alert the wider countryside. The first courier was a tanner named William Dawes, Jr. The second had already proved his value as a trusted messenger in nearly a dozen rides to New York, Philadelphia, New Hampshire, and, twice so far this month, Lexington and Concord. Paul Revere had often been mentioned in various newspapers over the past year because of the dispatches he carried from Boston. After a brief consultation with Warren, Revere hurried to his nearby house, snatched up his riding boots and a long overcoat, then picked his way through the twisting North End alleys to the waterfront. Two accomplices waited with a dinghy. Softly they rowed from the wharf.

In 1775, America had more than three thousand churches, representing eighteen denominations, but none was more important on this April night than Christ Church in Boston's Salem Street. Known as Old North, the church featured eight great bells cast in England, a magnificent quartet of hand-carved wooden angels perched above the nave, and a towering steeple, long used as a landmark by navigators entering the harbor. As carefully planned earlier in the week, another ally—Revere

PAUL REVERE'S RIDE AS DEPICTED IN THE PAINTING "AWAKEN..." [LOC]

identified him only as "a friend"—climbed 154 stairs and then a rickety ladder to a window in the steeple's north face, lugging two lanterns of tinned steel with glass panels and metal rings for hanging or carrying. Flint and steel soon lighted the candles, and twin gleams could be seen across the harbor. As Revere intended, rebel leaders across the Charles River now knew that British troops were moving across Back Bay—two if by sea—rather than taking the more roundabout, one-if-by-land route through Roxbury.

Handed the reins to a big brown New England mare, Revere swung into the saddle and took off at a canter across Charlestown Neck, her hooves striking sparks. Two hours later, he rode into Lexington, his horse sweating and foaming after outgalloping a pair of Gage's mounted watchmen near Charlestown. Along his route, Revere had alerted almost every farmstead and local minuteman captain within shouting distance.

A REIMAGINING OF THE MINUTEMEN ASSEMBLING ON APRIL 19, 1775, PUBLISHED BY A LOCAL PRINTMAKER IN 1876. [LOC]

The herald delivered his message to Adams and Hancock: British regulars by the hundreds were coming, first by boat, then on foot. There was not a moment to lose. Thirty minutes later, Dawes arrived with the same warning, and the two riders soon swung toward Concord, six miles away.

Now the Lexington bell began to clang in its wooden tower. More gallopers rode off to rouse half a hundred villages. Warning gunshots echoed from farm to farm. Bonfires flared. Drums beat. Across the colony solemn men grabbed their muskets and stalked off in search of danger. This day would be famous before it dawned.

THE BELLS IN THE TOWER AT LEXINGTON WARNED THE REBEL MILITIA OF APPROACHING BRITISH TROOPS. [LOC]

Lexington was occupied by 750 people and 400 cows. On the village green some 130 militiamen, summoned by the insistent pealing of the bell, milled about, stamping their feet against the nighttime chill. They awaited orders from their captain, John Parker. A scout dispatched in search of redcoats returned around 3:00 a.m. to advise Parker that none could be found.

Parker's scout had not ventured far enough east. The British making for Concord were there, the vanguard led by Major John Pitcairn, the marine commander in Boston. They were coming on hard, spurred by the distant popping of warning shots and the gleaming of alarm fires flaring on the horizon.

Soon after 4:00 a.m., the sounds of an alert countryside intensified—bells, shots, distant hoofbeats. Pitcairn ordered his troops to halt and load their weapons. The men surged forward, breathing hard, pulses pounding. The fourteen-inch bayonets on their muskets protruded above their heads like a picket fence.

The main British force was less than two miles from Lexington when another scout brought word to Captain Parker of their approach. The British vanguard swung into view in the early morning light. Three of the companies veered to the right of the meetinghouse at double-quick time. Pitcairn, on his horse, led the rest of the column to the left, before cantering onto the Common.

"Soldiers, don't fire," Pitcairn yelled, according to a British lieutenant. "Keep your ranks. Form and surround them." Spectators gawking from the road heard other officers yell, "Throw down your arms, ye villains, ye rebels!" and "Disperse, you rebels, immediately!" When British regulars closed to within fifty yards, Parker apparently took the command to heart. As he would say under oath a week later, "Upon their sudden approach, I immediately ordered our militia to disperse and not to fire."

IN THE FIRST SKIRMISH OF THE AMERICAN REVOLUTION, BRITISH TROOPS KILLED EIGHT AMERICAN MILITIAMEN AT LEXINGTON. *[LOC]*

A single gunshot sounded above the noise of moving men, possibly a warning or a sniper shot from the tavern. Whoever fired first on the Common would remain forever uncertain, but muskets quickly barked from the British line. Brilliant yellow flame erupted from British muzzles. The acrid smell of burning gunpowder rolled across the battlefield, punctuated by shrieks and the terrible thudding of bullets hitting flesh and bone. Few of Parker's men managed to fire more than once, if that.

In the end, Lexington had been not a battle or even a skirmish, but an execution. The only British casualties were two privates lightly wounded by gunshots and Pitcairn's horse, nicked twice in the flank. The American tally was far worse. Eight rebels were dead, nine wounded. Of those slain, only two bodies lay on the original American line. Several had taken bullets in the back while dispersing.

When the smoke cleared, the British formed again by companies and turned to march west, toward Concord.

FIVE

CONCORD, MASSACHUSETTS

April 19, 1775

Concord was ready for them. Paul Revere had been captured by a British mounted patrol at a bend in the road near Folly Pond, but William Dawes had managed to escape at a gallop. Revere was soon released, though without his brown mare. But others had carried warnings into Concord, where a lookout at the courthouse fired his musket and pulled on the bell rope. A clanging loud enough to wake the dead soon drove all 1,500 living souls from their beds.

Many families fled west or north, or into a secluded forest called Oaky Bottom, clutching the family Bible and a few place settings of silver while peering back to see if their houses were burning. Others buried their treasures in garden plots or lowered them down wells. Boys herded oxen and milk cows into the swamps, flicking at their haunches with switches. Militiamen, alone or in clusters or in entire companies with fife and drum, rambled toward Concord, carrying pine torches and bullet pouches, their pockets stuffed with rye bread and cheese. "It seemed as if men came down from the clouds," a witness recalled.

Sometime before 8:00 a.m., perhaps two hundred impatient militiamen headed for Lexington to the rap of drums and the trill of fifes. Twenty minutes later, eight hundred British soldiers came into view barely a quarter mile away. "The sun shined on their arms & they made a noble appearance in their red coats," a nineteen-year-old minuteman later testified. "We retreated." Colonel James Barrett, the militia commander, ordered them to make for better ground on the ridgeline a mile north, across the Concord River. Concord village was given over to the enemy.

A CONTEMPORARY DRAWING SHOWS BRITISH REGULARS MARCHING THROUGH CONCORD AS THEIR OFFICERS WATCH FOR REBELS. [NYPL]

Into largely deserted Concord the British regulars marched, in search of feed for the officers' horses and water for the parched men. Gage's late intelligence had been accurate: In recent weeks, most military stores in Concord had been moved to nine other villages or into deeper holes in the mud and manure. Regulars seized sixty barrels of flour found in a gristmill, smashing them open and powdering the streets. They tossed five hundred pounds of musket balls into a pond, chopped down the liberty pole (a symbol of resistance to British rule), and eventually made a bonfire

VILLAGERS RAISING A LIBERTY POLE, WHILE DISGRUNTLED LOYALISTS IN THE CROWD WATCH. *[LOC]*

of gun carriages, spare wheels, tent pegs, and a stockpile of wooden spoons.

Since 1654, a bridge had spanned the Concord River just north of the village. Seven British companies crossed the bridge around nine o'clock that Wednesday morning. Three companies remained to guard it, while the other four continued with Captain Lawrence Parsons to a nearby farm, where they would again be disappointed in their search for feed for their horses and water for the men.

The five Concord militia companies had taken post on Punkatasset Hill, a gentle slope half a mile north of the bridge. Two companies from Lincoln, two more from Bedford, and one minute company from Acton joined them, bringing their numbers to perhaps 450, enough to overwhelm the hundred or so redcoats peering up from the road.

On the order, the Americans loaded their muskets and walked downhill to within three hundred yards of the enemy. Without orders, a British soldier fired into the river. The white splash rose as if from a thrown stone. More shots followed, a spattering of musketry from both sides that built into a ragged volley. Battle smoke draped the river. Three minutes of gunplay cost five American casualties, including two dead. For the British, eight were wounded and two killed, but another badly hurt soldier, trying to regain his feet, was mortally wounded by minuteman Ammi White, who crushed his skull with a hatchet.

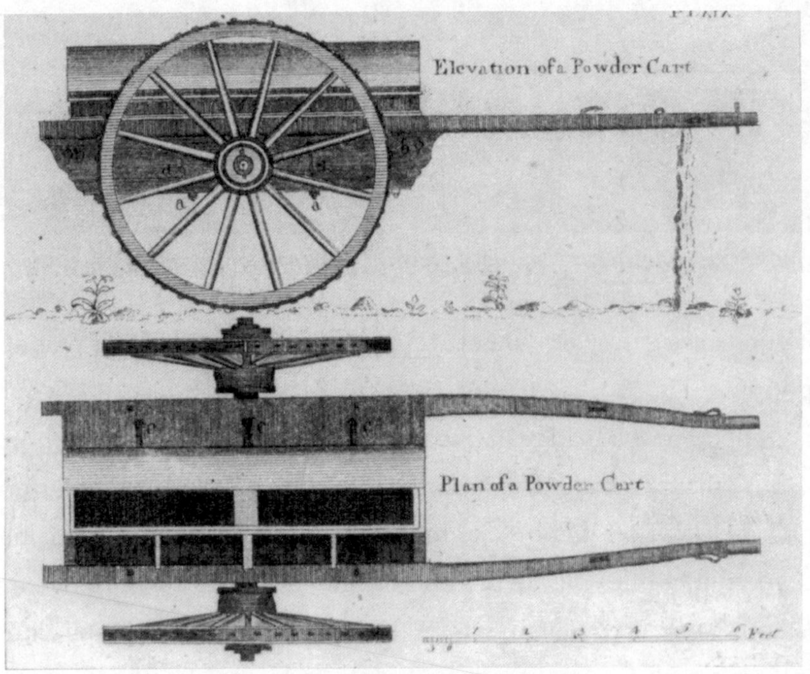

A CART USED TO CARRY GUNPOWDER. *[LOC]*

The British were outnumbered and outgunned. No fife and drum would play as they began the walk back to Boston. Badly wounded privates would be left to rebel mercy, but horse-drawn carriages for injured officers were wheeled out from Concord's barns and stables. Companies again arranged themselves in marching order and a final round of food and brandy was tossed back. Before noon the red procession headed east, silent and somber, every man aware that eighteen miles of danger lay ahead.

Using tactics practiced during years of combat in North American woodlands, British light infantry flankers swept to the right and left of the troops through the tilled fields and apple orchards, stumbling over frost-heaved rocks while searching for ambushers. The rebels were there, though well concealed. They could be seen running behind outbuildings and across the pastures and meadows. British soldiers wheeled and fired. Now the running gun battle began in earnest, with crackling musketry and spurts of smoke and flame. The American ranks swelled to a thousand, twelve hundred, fifteen hundred, more by the hour. The combat grew even more ferocious and intimate when the British regulars were still thirteen miles from Boston Harbor. Some British soldiers started to straggle, although officers tried to force the men back into formation.

And then, like a crimson vision, more than a thousand redcoats appeared on a hill half a mile east, sent from Boston as reinforcements. Heavy musket fire and the first British cannonballs kept the militiamen at bay. Still, the British regulars continued their retreat. Ambush was possible at every corner. Men on both sides were wounded and died at many spots along the road. The final miles to Charlestown were agonizing—casualties climbing, ammunition dwindling, sun sinking, men at the last pitch of exhaustion.

The shooting ebbed and finally faded away, along with this very long day. Brigadier Hugh Earl Percy, who led the reinforcements, ordered the grenadiers and light infantry to the Charlestown wharves, where boat crews waited to row them the half mile to Boston. Five hundred fresh regulars arrived to guard the heights below Charlestown Neck, including Bunker Hill.

The first of the war's 1,300 actions had been fought, the first battle deaths mourned. Fifty-eight towns and villages, from Acton to

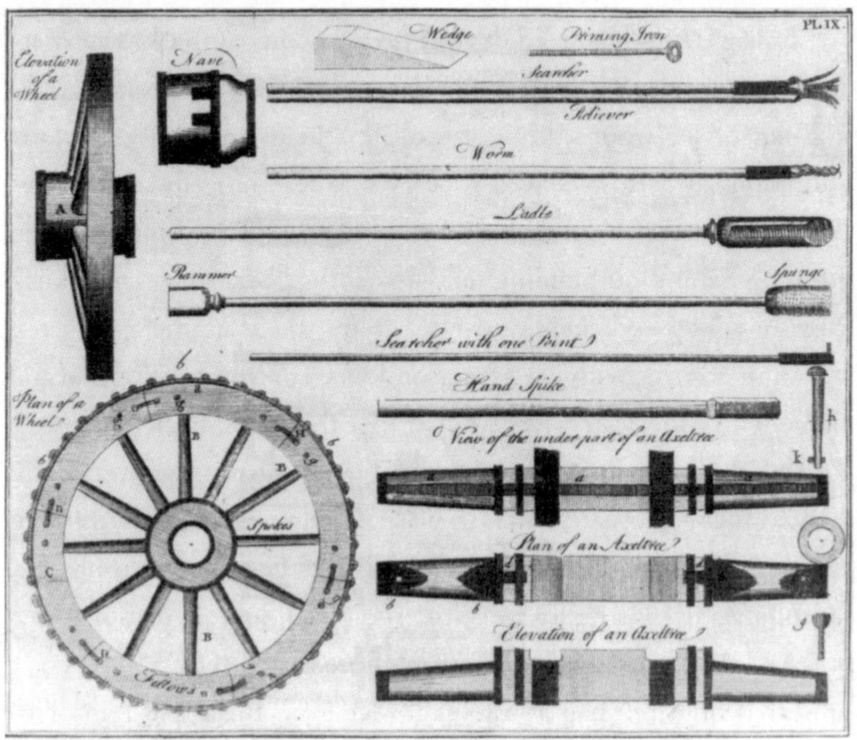

TOOLS USED TO FIRE A CANNON AND THE PARTS OF A WHEELED ARTILLERY CARRIAGE USED TO MOVE THE BIG GUN. *[LOC]*

Woburn, had sent men into the fight; fourteen thousand had marched against the British regulars, of whom about four thousand came in close contact with the British column. For all the chaos of the day, the Americans had demonstrated impressive organizational skills.

Like a burning fuse, accounts of that day raced across New England and down the Atlantic seaboard. "To arms!" messengers cried. "Gage has fired upon the people!" In barely three weeks, the first reports of the day's action would reach Charleston and Savannah, a thousand miles south. Lurid rumors spread quickly: of grandfathers shot in their beds, of families burned alive, of women bayoneted. Americans in thirteen colonies were alarmed, aroused, and angry.

A swift American schooner, the *Quero*, sailed from Salem, Massachusetts, for England on April 29, carrying recent copies of the *Essex Gazette*, with an article that began, "Last Wednesday, the 19th of April, the Troops of his Britannick Majesty commenced Hostilities upon the People of this Province." The king's resolve was unshaken. He still believed that "with firmness and perseverance America will be brought to submission."

In the colonies, preparations for war were beginning. Citizens retrieved cannons and musket balls from millponds, thickets, and various hiding places. Shoes from dead horses and pewter spoons were melted down to become bullets.

SIX

BUNKER HILL, BOSTON, MASSACHUSETTS

May–June 1775

In late April, the provincial congress in Massachusetts called for thirty thousand American troops to turn out, and men left farms, shops, and families. Two thousand were said to march from New Hampshire. Forty-six of Connecticut's seventy-two towns sent men, and classes at Yale College were canceled for lack of students. "The ardor of our people is such that they can't be kept back," a committee in New Haven, Connecticut, informed John Hancock. Houses in Cambridge abandoned by families loyal to the king were confiscated for use as barracks and officers' headquarters. Eleven hundred tents accumulated by the Committee of Supply sprouted along the Charles, and a request went out to sailmakers and shipmasters for more. "We have stripped the seaports of canvas to make tents," a member of the provincial congress reported.

No sooner did the grand American army gather than it began to melt away. Farmers left to tend their spring fields, shopkeepers to tend their counters. Most Connecticut troops soon wandered

JOHN HANCOCK. *[LOC]*

home, discouraged by the shortages of food and drink around Boston. The force would dwindle to sixteen thousand or so within a month of the shots at Lexington, although no one was sure of the number.

Shortages extended beyond canvas and rations. "We are in want of almost everything, but of nothing so much as arms and ammunition," Joseph Warren wrote on May 15 to Philadelphia, where the Second Continental Congress had just convened. Massachusetts counted thirty-eight cannons, mostly inferior iron guns. Rhode Island sent a few brass fieldpieces, but they were hardly sufficient to confront the British empire.

In midmonth, welcome news arrived from Lake Champlain in New York, more than two hundred miles northwest: At 3:30 a.m. on May 10, eighty-five whooping New England roughnecks who called themselves the Green Mountain Boys had swarmed from a flat-bottomed boat, called a bateau, to overrun the British garrison at Fort Ticonderoga in New York. Almost fifty sleepy redcoats had surrendered without a fight, as had a smaller detachment at nearby Fort Crown Point. Two men led the raid in an unsteady partnership: a sometime farmer, lead miner, and philosopher named Ethan Allen and a gifted apothecary, trader, and hothead named Benedict Arnold. The captured booty included some two hundred iron cannons, ten tons of musket balls, and thirty thousand musket flints. The victories also gave the Americans control not only of Ticonderoga—the most strategic inland position on the continent—but also of Lake Champlain, the traditional invasion route into, or out of, Canada.

ETHAN ALLEN, WITH HIS SWORD RAISED, DURING THE CAPTURE OF FORT TICONDEROGA. [LOC]

From his headquarters, General Gage awaited reinforcements and braced for a rebel assault. Regiments built several small batteries on the Common and a larger redoubt on Beacon Hill. Gunners at Boston Neck were ordered to keep lighted matches by their cannons at all times. Regulars patrolled the wharves every half hour. Loyalist volunteers kept vigil in the streets at night. "We are threatened with great multitudes," Gage wrote in mid-May. "The people called friends of government are few."

Gage declared martial law on June 12 with a long, windy denunciation of "the infatuated multitudes." He offered to pardon those who "lay down their arms and return to the duties of peaceable subjects." Some regulars longed for a decisive battle; "taking the bull by the horns" became an oft-heard phrase in the regiments. "I wish the Americans may be brought to a sense of their duty," an officer wrote in mid-June. "One good drubbing, which

I long to give them . . . might have a good effect." The imminent arrival of transport ships with light dragoons, more marines, and several foot regiments would bring the British garrison to over six thousand troops, not enough to subdue Massachusetts, much less the continent, but sufficient, as Gage told London, to "make an attempt upon some of the rebel posts, which becomes every day more necessary." Two desirable patches of high ground around Boston remained unfortified, and Gage knew from an informant that American commanders had their eyes on the same slopes: the elevation beyond Boston Neck known as the Dorchester Heights, and, across the Charles River, the high terrain above Charlestown called Bunker, or Bunker's, Hill.

A British battle plan was made to seize the former on Sunday, June 18, with a bombardment of nearby Roxbury village while the rebels were at church, followed by the construction of two fortifications on the heights. If all went well, regulars could then capture the high ground on the Charlestown peninsula and eventually attack the American encampment at Cambridge. No sooner was the plan conceived than it was leaked to the rebel Committee of Safety;

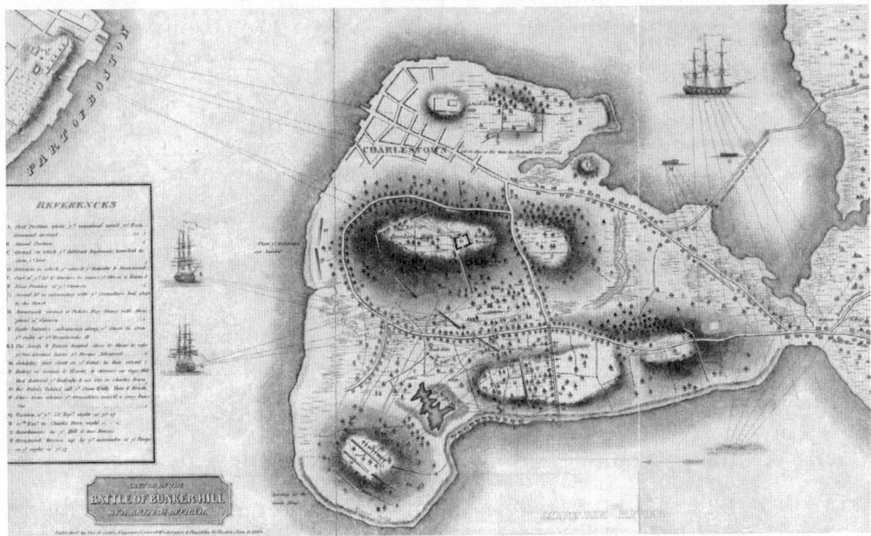

A BRITISH MAP SHOWING THE ATTACK DURING THE BATTLE OF BUNKER HILL. [NYPL]

British officers seemed incapable of keeping their mouths shut in a town full of American spies and eavesdroppers.

Meeting in Hastings House, a mansion near the Cambridge Common, the Committee of Safety on June 15 voted unanimously that "the hill called Bunker's Hill in Charlestown be securely kept and defended."

The American camps bustled. Arms and ammunition were inspected, with each marching soldier to carry thirty rounds of ammunition. A note to the Committee of Supply advised that "the army is destitute of shirts & trousers, and if any [are] in store, pray they may be sent." Liquor sales stopped. Teamsters carted the books and scientific instruments from Harvard's library to Andover for safekeeping. Organ pipes were yanked from the Anglican church and melted down for musket bullets. An equipment storehouse issued all forty-eight shovels in stock as well as ammunition to selected regiments—typically forty or fifty pounds of powder, a thousand balls, and a few hundred flints.

Shortly after 6:00 p.m. on Friday, June 16, three Massachusetts regiments drifted onto the Cambridge Common. They wore the usual homespun linen shirts and breeches tinted with walnut or sumac dye. Most carried a blanket or bedroll, many with a strap across the forehead to support the weight on their backs. A clergyman's benediction droned over their bowed heads, and with a final amen they replaced their low-crowned hats and turned east down the Charlestown road.

The column was led by a trim, blue-eyed colonel wearing a blue coat with a single row of buttons and a tricorne hat. Colonel William Prescott of Pepperell, Massachusetts, had fought twice in Canada during wars against the French, earning a reputation for cool self-possession under fire. In this war, he reportedly had vowed

COLONEL WILLIAM PRESCOTT. *[NYPL]*

never to be taken alive. "He was a bold man," one soldier later wrote of him, "and gave his orders like a bold man."

Prescott ordered the column to continue southeast. Colonel Richard Gridley quickly staked out a site for an earthen redoubt—an imperfect square with sides about 130 feet long—not on nearly impregnable Bunker Hill, as the Committee of Safety had specified, but on the southwest slope of pastureland to be known as Breed's Hill. No one seemed certain why this spot was chosen. But, accustomed to pick-and-shovel work, the men grabbed tools from the carts and began hacking at the hillside.

The rhythmic chink of metal on hard ground carried to the *Lively*, one of the warships in the British squadron now anchored next to the Charlestown ferry way. As light seeped across the eastern horizon at 4:00 a.m. on Saturday, June 17, the graveyard watch officer on the vessel strained to decipher the odd sounds above the groaning

COLONEL WILLIAM PRESCOTT AND HIS COMRADES BYPASS BUNKER HILL TO TAKE POSITIONS ON BREED'S HILL. *[NYPL]*

of the ship's masts and the Charles River whispering along her hull. He summoned the captain, whose spyglass soon showed hundreds of tiny dark figures tearing at the distant slope with spades and pickaxes.

Sailors were called to action. They tumbled from their hammocks, feet slapping across the deck as they ran to their battle stations. A shouted command carried across the gun deck, and tongues of flame burst from the ship in a broadside of nine-pounders. Gunners swabbed the smoking barrels, rammed home powder and shot, and another flock of iron balls flew toward Breed's Hill. Other British ships eventually joined in—*Glasgow*, *Symmetry*, *Falcon*, *Spitfire*, more than seventy guns all told—along with twenty-four-pounders from the Copp's Hill battery in Boston's North End.

On Breed's Hill, screaming cannonballs streaked overhead or punched into the hillside, smashing two barrels containing the American water supply. "The danger we were in made us think there was treachery, & that we were brought here to be all slain," a young American militiaman would write to his mother in Rhode Island.

The deep boom of *Lively*'s broadsides had wakened General Gage, as it woke all of Boston. His headquarters at Province House soon bustled with red uniforms. After conferring with his senior officers, Gage chose a direct assault to be led by William Howe, the senior major general in Boston. Ten companies of light infantry and grenadiers would muster at Long Wharf, bolstered by several other regiments. The remaining light infantry and grenadiers, backed by additional regiments, would embark from North Battery, with other marines and regulars in reserve. Gage ended the conference with a stark order: "Any man who shall quit his ranks on any pretense, or shall dare to plunder or pillage, will be executed without mercy."

With a clatter of boots across the floor, officers hurried down the hall and out the door to prepare their commands for battle.

As the morning ticked by, *Glasgow* and *Symmetry* hammered Charlestown Neck from an anchorage west of the peninsula. Shortly before noon, as heat began to build in Boston, long columns of regulars tramped to fife and drum through the town's cobbled streets from the Common to the docks. At one thirty, twenty-eight boats carrying 1,200 soldiers pulled away from Long Wharf.

At the same time, the most critical rebel reinforcements reached Charlestown Neck: hundreds of long-striding New Hampshire militiamen commanded by Colonel John Stark. Crossing the narrow isthmus shortly after 2:00 p.m., harassed with shot from Royal Navy guns, the Hampshiremen ascended Bunker Hill at a deliberate pace, then descended to the northeast lip of the peninsula. A quick glance disclosed the American peril: Though Colonel Prescott continued to improve his imperfect fort, his position could still be outflanked by redcoats advancing up the Mystic River shoreline. To block the narrow, muddy beach, Stark's men scooted down the eight-foot riverbank and quickly stacked fieldstones to build a short, stout wall. Other Hampshiremen took positions behind the livestock fence to extend Captain Thomas Knowlton's line, stuffing it with hay, grass, and stray fence rails. Sixty musketmen arranged themselves on the beach in a triple row behind the new barricade. There they awaited their enemy.

Landing at Morton's Point with the second lift of six hundred infantry and artillery troops from North Battery, General Howe climbed a nearby hillock as gunners shouldered their fieldpieces onto dry ground and the empty boats rowed back to Boston. "It

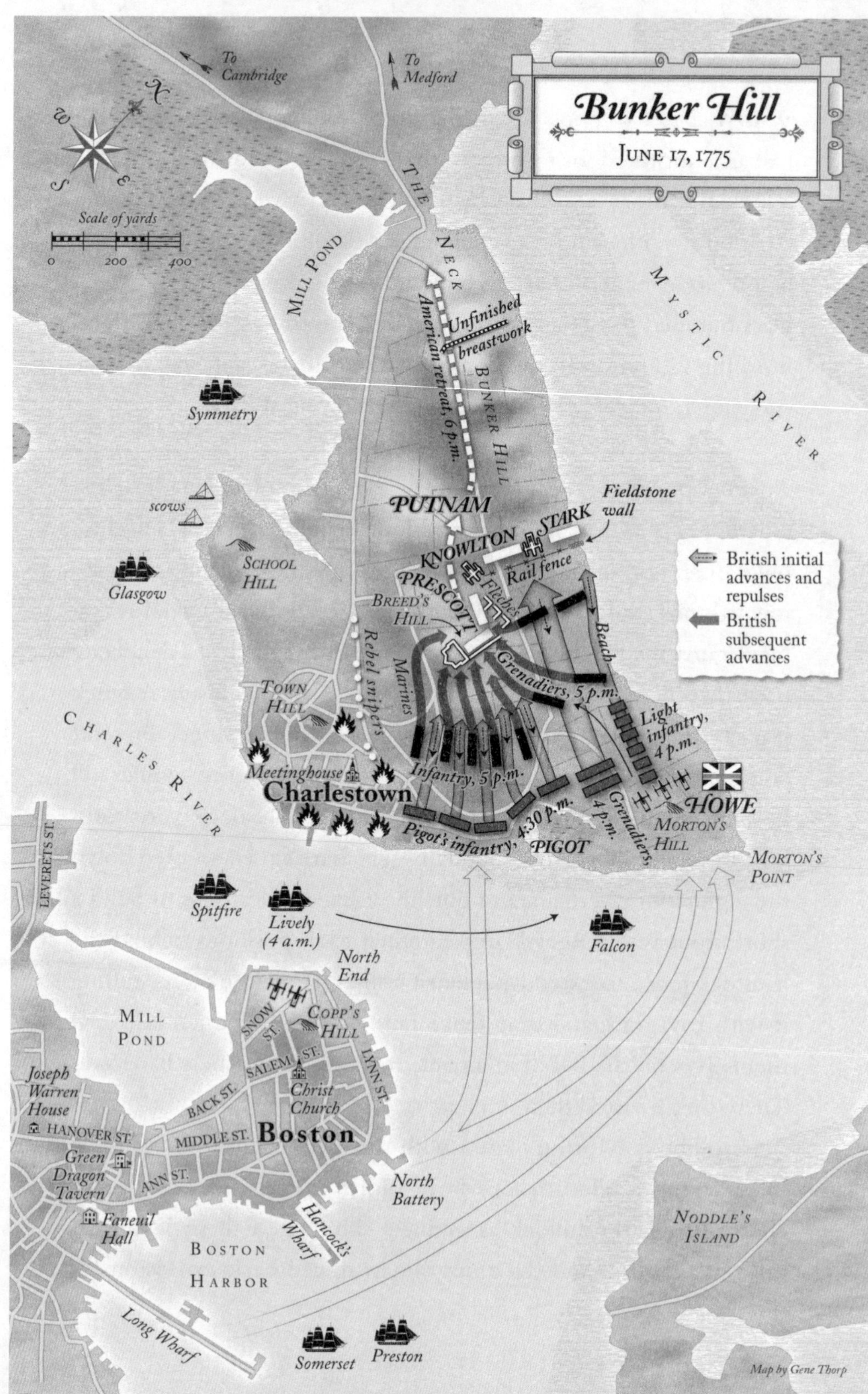
Bunker Hill
June 17, 1775
To Cambridge
To Medford
The Neck
Mill Pond
Scale of yards
0
200
400
Unfinished breastwork
American retreat, 6 p.m.
Bunker Hill
Mystic River
Symmetry
scows
Putnam
Fieldstone wall
Knowlton
Stark
School Hill
Glasgow
Prescott
Rail fence
Flèches
Breed's Hill
Rebel snipers
Marines
Beach
British initial advances and repulses
British subsequent advances
Grenadiers, 5 p.m.
Town Hill
Light infantry, 4 p.m.
Charles River
Meetinghouse
Infantry, 5 p.m.
Charlestown
Howe
Pigot's infantry, 4:30 p.m.
Grenadiers, 4 p.m.
Pigot
Morton's Hill
Morton's Point
Leverets St.
Spitfire
Lively (4 a.m.)
Falcon
North End
Mill Pond
Snow St.
Copp's Hill
Salem St.
Lynn St.
Joseph Warren House
Christ Church
Back St.
Hanover St.
Middle St.
Boston
Green Dragon Tavern
Ann St.
North Battery
Faneuil Hall
Hancock's Wharf
Noddle's Island
Boston Harbor
Long Wharf
Somerset
Preston
Map by Gene Thorp

BRITISH TROOPS MOVE TOWARD AMERICAN FORTIFICATIONS ON BREED'S HILL. *[LOC]*

was instantly perceived the enemy were very strongly posted," he subsequently told London.

Howe made his plan. The Mystic beach seemed a promising corridor from which to outflank and turn the rebel line. On foot, the general would personally lead the British right wing. The left wing, led by the diminutive Brigadier General Robert Pigot, would attack the redoubt to fix the enemy in place and maybe even storm it once Howe's troops had broken through.

On order, the great mass of redcoats heaved forward with a clatter of equipment and more bawled commands. "Push on!" the troops yelled. "Push on!" Watching as this red tide advanced, Captain Ebenezer Bancroft of Dunstable, Massachusetts, would give voice to every patriot on the battlefield: "It was an awful moment."

The moment grew more awful. For two months, Vice Admiral Samuel Graves, commander of the North American station, had longed to rain destruction on rebel heads. The admiral arrived on the battlefield by barge to note the hazard that enemy snipers in

Charlestown posed to Pigot's left flank. Did General Howe wish "to have the place burned?" Graves asked. As a precaution, brick furnaces aboard several warships had prepared all morning to heat cannonballs. Indeed, General Howe did wish it so.

Gunners loaded combustible shells, known as carcasses, each packed with gunpowder, Swedish pitch, saltpeter, and tallow. The Charlestown meetinghouse, with its slender, towering steeple, provided a conspicuous target. The first shell fell short, bursting near the ferry slip. Gunners corrected their elevation, and within minutes the meetinghouse was in flames. Taverns, the courthouse, stores and warehouses, distilleries and tanneries soon followed.

FOUR BRITISH WARSHIPS AND AN ARTILLERY BATTERY ON COPP'S HILL IN BOSTON SET FIRE TO CHARLESTOWN DURING THE BATTLE OF BUNKER HILL. [LOC]

The rebels waited, now killing-mad. At 4:00 p.m., well over two thousand regulars ascended the slope in two divisions. In the redoubt, Prescott angrily waved his sword to rebuke several musketmen who were firing at impossible ranges; they were to wait until the enemy was danger-close, within a hundred feet or so. Stark told his men to hold fire until they could see the regulars' gaiters below their knees.

Beyond a slight curve in the Mystic shoreline stood Colonel Stark's newly built fieldstone wall, defended by a few dozen rebel musketmen, some kneeling with their gun barrels resting on the stones. Closing at a trot to within fifty yards, redcoats from the 23rd Royal Welch Fusiliers at the front of the column lowered their bayonets and prepared to charge. A stupendous, searing volley ripped into the British ranks, blowing the fusiliers off their feet. With a third of the Welch Fusiliers wounded, mortally or otherwise, the King's Own Light Infantry behind them surged forward; they, too, were slaughtered, followed by the 10th Foot, the 52nd Foot, and other light companies trailing them. After a final, futile surge, the regulars turned and ran "in a very great disorder," a witness reported.

Howe heard the commotion below the riverbank to his right, but the rail fence just ahead, stiff with hundreds of American gunmen, drew his full attention. As he and the grenadiers took another stride, the top rail erupted in musket flame and filthy smoke, quickly followed by a volley from the rebel second rank. "The whole line was one blaze," a young militiaman from Sudbury, Massachusetts, later recalled. "They fell in heaps, actually in heaps . . . The bodies lay there very thick." Howe pulled his men back briefly to regroup, then surged forward again, only to be smashed once more. At last, Howe turned and trudged down the hill, unhurt himself, though his white stockings were red with British blood.

Brigadier Pigot had suffered few casualties in moving toward the redoubt. But now the weight of the British assault necessarily shifted to his men. Marines, three army regiments, and various detached companies pressed toward the crest of Breed's Hill, bedeviled by fences and stone walls. Volley upon volley crashed from the redoubt and the protruding breastwork so that "the enemy fell like grass when mowed," a rebel fifer said.

Bloodied but unbowed, William Howe drew up a new plan. With more than five hundred reserve troops preparing to cross the Charles River from Boston, he would renew the attack on the redoubt by shifting two regiments and the surviving grenadiers from his own corps to Pigot's on the left. Peering over the parapet from his battered redoubt, Colonel Prescott watched the red tide again creep up the Breed's Hill pastureland. The 150 or so Americans remaining in his small fort—their faces blackened by soot and powder—had little ammunition left. Militiamen searched pockets for stray cartridges or tapped the final grains from powder horns, tearing strips from their shirttails to use for packing. Prescott ordered the last artillery cartridges torn open and the loose powder distributed to his infantry.

The failure of the rebel headquarters to resupply the redoubt from the Massachusetts military stores was almost as disheartening as the scarcity of reinforcements. Hundreds of leaderless militiamen "in great confusion" ambled about on Bunker Hill or beyond the Neck. Men cowered behind apple trees; others behind rocks or haycocks. Others were simply retreating.

When Pigot's legions again drew near, the battle turned. American gunshots grew scattered. Angry redcoats tumbled into the redoubt, shooting and stabbing furiously. At the end, thirty American bodies lay scattered across the area. The triumphant, vengeful roar of British regulars could be heard in Boston.

Casualties were brutal. Through Saturday night and all day Sunday, wagons, carriages, sedan chairs, wood carts, and wheelbarrows hauled broken men to makeshift hospitals, barracks, and rooming houses—the British to Boston and the rebels to Cambridge.

THE DEATH OF JOSEPH WARREN, A NEWLY APPOINTED AMERICAN GENERAL, AT THE BATTLE OF BUNKER HILL. *[LOC]*

American casualties approached 450, including 138 dead, but the British toll was much worse, with more than 1,000 killed or wounded.

To many American fighters, the battle now called Bunker Hill felt like defeat. Ground had been surrendered to the enemy, the peninsula lost. Many were furious that militiamen had retreated. The burning of Charlestown, the first of several American towns to be obliterated during the war, stirred both sorrow and rage. A survey found that 232 houses, 95 barns, 76 shops, 25 warehouses, a dozen mills, 81 miscellaneous buildings, and 17 wharves had burned. But this rebel force that lacked not only sufficient ammunition and field artillery but also combat reserves, a coherent chain of command, and even water had made an impression on their adversaries.

In a letter to the British government in London on June 26,

Gage wrote, "These people . . . are now spirited up by a rage and enthusiasm as great as ever people were possessed of." He continued, "You must proceed in earnest or give the business up. The loss we have sustained is greater than we can bear. Small armies can't afford such losses . . . I wish this cursed place was burned."

SEVEN

CAMBRIDGE CAMP, CAMBRIDGE, MASSACHUSETTS

July–October 1775

It was possible that not one of the soldiers now under his command in Massachusetts knew what George Washington of Virginia looked like. Few Americans did. Imaginary portraits that bore no resemblance to him had been printed in the newspapers after his unanimous selection by the Continental Congress seventeen days earlier to be "general and commander-in-chief of the American forces," an army to be known as the Continental Army. Now, on July 2, 1775, a rainy Sunday, here he was in the flesh, trotting past the sodden sentries just after noon with a small escort and baggage that included a stack of books on generalship and a volume with diagrams on how to build fortifications and otherwise run a war.

A PORTRAIT OF GEORGE WASHINGTON. *[LOC]*

Washington's reputation preceded him. As a twenty-three-year-old colonel commanding Virginia's provincial forces in the last French war, he survived four bullets through his uniform and another through his hat and had two horses shot dead beneath him before dragging his mortally wounded commander across the river and riding sixty miles for help. That ordeal gave Washington an aura of indestructibility while convincing him that "the all-powerful dispensations of Providence" had protected him "beyond all human probability."

Washington needed little time to grasp the lay of the land. His mahogany-and-brass spyglass showed two armies barely a mile apart. The enemy was "strongly entrenched on Bunker's Hill," their white tents covering the land and three floating batteries in the river. Washington's own troops occupied more than 230 buildings from Cambridge to Brookline, two dozen of which were used as hospitals. The enemy's strength was reckoned at 11,500—almost twice the number Gage actually had fit for duty. "Between you and me," Washington wrote to a Virginia friend, "I think we are in an exceedingly dangerous situation."

Commands poured from his headquarters. For every moment when Washington drew his sword or spurred his horse to the sound of the guns, there would be a thousand administrative moments: dictating orders, scribbling letters, convening meetings, badgering, praising, mediating. He quickly saw that, unlike the fantasy army that existed in congressional imaginations, this army was woefully unskilled, lacked artillery and engineering expertise, and was led by few officers with extensive combat experience.

Even as he immersed himself in tactical details, Washington recognized that a commander in chief must be a capable strategist; that spyglass had to focus on the horizon as much as on the local battlefield. War, he knew, was a struggle of political wills. And Washington was—instinctively, brilliantly—a political general: In the month following his departure from Philadelphia, he wrote seven letters to Congress, acknowledging its superior authority while maneuvering to get what he needed.

AN IMAGINED SCENE OF GENERAL GEORGE WASHINGTON TAKING COMMAND OF THE CONTINENTAL ARMY IN JULY 1775. [LOC]

What he had under his command were mostly very young men. Most could read but did not have much formal schooling. Some joined for the money—a private was paid six and two-thirds dollars a month, more than a young man could make working as a farm laborer. Few had uniforms, they were mostly quite dirty, and they had yet to be taught how to be soldiers. No two companies marched alike. For hours and days on end, Washington rode from Chelsea to Roxbury and back—inspecting, correcting, fuming—then returned to headquarters to issue another raft of detailed, encouraging commands. In the three months following his arrival in Cambridge, the commander in chief on five occasions condemned excessive drinking. Four times he demanded better hygiene. Thirteen times he pleaded for accurate reports from subordinate commanders to gauge the size and health of the army. Company rolls were to be called twice daily, and orders read aloud to ensure comprehension, if not obedience. No man was to appear on sentry duty who was "not perfectly sober and tolerably observing," nor was anyone to appear in formation "without having on his stockings and shoes." Fines were levied: a shilling for swearing, two shillings sixpence for unauthorized gunplay.

"My greatest concern is to establish order, regularity & discipline," Washington wrote to John Hancock, president of the Continental Congress. "My difficulties thicken every day." In truth, this immensely wealthy man with a huge estate in Virginia and scores of enslaved people to tend his business in his absence could hardly comprehend the sacrifice made by most of his men in leaving their families, shops, and farms in high season. For that vital link between commander and commanded to be welded solidly, Washington would have to know in his bones—and the men would have to know that he knew—what was risked and what was lost in serving at his side.

Aggressive and even reckless, Washington longed for a decisive, bloody battle that would cause Britain to lose heart and sue for a political settlement. That appeared unlikely in Boston, where "it is almost impossible for us to get to them," he wrote. Instead, the summer and fall would be limited to skirmishes, raids, and sniping. Washington could not begin to plan to wage a long campaign, given that his army was short of virtually everything an army needed:

camp kettles, shovels and axes, cartridge boxes, straw, bowls, spoons. Simply finding enough food for the regiments around Boston had become difficult.

But no shortage was as dangerous as that discovered in early August. Washington's staff calculated that an army of twenty thousand men, in thirty-nine regiments with a hundred cannons, required two thousand barrels of gunpowder—a hundred tons. Powder was the one essential. Each pound contained enough for a volley from forty-eight muskets. A big cannon throwing a thirty-two-pound ball required eleven or twelve pounds of powder per shot; an eighteen-pounder used six or seven pounds. A survey taken soon after Washington's arrival reported 303 barrels in his magazines, or fifteen tons—enough to stave off a British attack, but too little for heavy cannon fire. "We are so exceedingly destitute," he told Hancock, "that our artillery will be of little use."

GEORGE WASHINGTON FRAMED BY PATRIOTIC IMAGERY, INCLUDING CANNONS, PISTOLS, FLAGS, AND AN EAGLE. [LOC]

A rebel schooner from Santo Domingo, in the West Indies, sailed up the Delaware River in late July under a false French flag with almost seven tons of smuggled gunpowder hidden in the hold beneath molasses barrels. Loaded into a half dozen wagons, the powder was promptly sent north with an armed escort. A second consignment of five tons soon followed, and by late August, Washington had enough for twenty-five rounds per soldier, still a meager amount. War could not be waged with an occasional smuggled windfall, yet not a single American powder mill existed when the rebellion began.

The American force exceeded twenty thousand by early November, but those present and fit for duty remained below fourteen thousand. To build morale, wrestling matches were staged. Men hunted for chestnuts, apples, and turnips in the countryside; they sang camp songs. No one doubted that winter was coming. The army would need ten thousand cords of firewood in the next few months, and Washington was already fretting over "a most mortifying scarcity" that hindered recruiting and could force his regiments to disband or risk freezing.

Every day British fire hit the camps, sometimes forty or fifty cannonballs for each American shot. Washington had little choice but to save his gunpowder, stockpile firewood, and launch an occasional raid or sniping attack with the ten companies of riflemen Congress had sent from Virginia, Maryland, and Pennsylvania.

EIGHT

FALMOUTH, MAINE

October 16, 1775

The American siege of Boston continued. In September, the British general Gage had been recalled. General William Howe was installed as commander in chief of the British colonies in America. Howe also had ration problems. He had eleven thousand mouths to feed and little to feed them with. "Starve them out" had been a Continental rallying cry since April. British supply contractors were supposed to stockpile at least a six-month food reserve in Boston, yet when Howe took command, there was less than a thirty-day supply.

LIEUTENANT GENERAL WILLIAM HOWE, THE NEW BRITISH COMMANDER IN CHIEF. [LOC]

✦✦✦

Four small British warships and a storeship sailed into Casco Bay off Falmouth, Maine, on the mild, breezy morning of Monday, October 16. Nearly two thousand souls lived in remote Falmouth, a hundred miles up the coast from Boston, the men scratching out a living as fishermen, millers, and lumberjacks.

For more than half a century, Royal Navy agents had routinely come to collect enormous white pines, some of them three feet in diameter and marked with the king's proprietary insignia. After felling, the great sticks were hauled into the water by twenty yokes of oxen, then lashed into rafts or raised onto ships and hauled across the Atlantic to Portsmouth, England, and other shipyards to be shaped as the towering masts on the king's biggest men-of-war. To the lament of British shipwrights, that mast trade had all but ended with the gunplay at Lexington. Felled timber had been hidden upriver from Falmouth, and after armed rebels twice thwarted British efforts to secure the masts, Royal Navy officers threatened "to beat the town down about their ears."

TALL WOODEN MASTS SUPPORT THE SAILS OF BRITISH MEN OF WAR. [LOC

At 4:00 p.m., a British naval officer with a marine escort rowed to the King Street dock, marched to the crowded town hall, and with a flourish delivered a written ultimatum. The decree warned that in the name of "the best of sovereigns . . . you have been guilty of the most unpardonable rebellion." The flotilla had orders to administer "a just punishment": Falmouth was given two hours to evacuate "the human species out of the said town." "Every heart," a clergyman wrote, "was seized with terror, every countenance changed color, and a profound silence ensued." A three-man delegation of townsmen rowed out to the British warship *Canceaux* to beg mercy of Lieutenant Henry Mowat, the flotilla commander.

Mowat's orders were firm. But because of "the known humanity of the British nation," he would hold his fire if by 8:00 a.m. the next day all small arms, ammunition, and the five carriage guns known to be in Falmouth were surrendered. All night long the townsfolk debated, fretted, wailed, and debated some more. Horse and ox teams plodded

NINE

CANADA

September 1775–January 1776

Some 230 miles northwest of Boston, a second siege now threatened Britain's hold on Canada. For almost a month, more than a thousand American troops had surrounded Fort St. Johns, a damp compound twenty miles below Montreal on the swampy western bank of the Richelieu River. By mid-October, seven hundred people were trapped at St. Johns, among them most of the British troops in Canada as well as most of the Royal Artillery's gunners, eighty women and children, and more than seventy Canadian volunteers.

THE CANADIAN CITY OF MONTREAL, VIEWED ACROSS THE ST. LAWRENCE RIVER. [LOC]

through Queen, Fish, and Middle shop goods, and the infirm. Hotheaded town themselves if Falmouth complied w old muskets were rowed out to the *Canceau* the people of Falmouth screwed up their co delegation to inform Mowat that they had "res deliver up the cannon and other arms." "Perceivin dren still in the town," Mowat later told Admiral G forty minutes after nine before the signal was hoisted.'

A red flag appeared on *Canceaux*'s main mast. Tong and flame abruptly licked from the ships' gun decks. Th shattered glass and splintered wood echoed along the wa where a dozen local trading boats also came under bombard For three hours fires blazed up, only to be swatted out by homeow ers and shopkeepers. But Britain would murder another America town. The *Essex Gazette* tallied 416 buildings destroyed, including 136 houses, the Episcopal church, various barns, the meetinghouse, the customs house, the library, and the new courthouse. Many of the hundred structures still standing were shot through by balls and shells, and the three-day rain that began at 10:00 p.m. ruined furnishings that had failed to burn.

A BRITISH SQUADRON COMMANDED BY CAPTAIN HENRY MOWAT ATTACKS FALMOUTH, MAINE, BURNING THE TOWN. [LOC]

The British regulars inside the fort still wore summer uniforms and suffered from the cold: The first hard frost had arrived on September 30, followed by eight consecutive days of rain. Some ripped the skirts from their coats to wrap around their feet. The garrison now lived on half rations and shared a total of twenty blankets, with no bedding or straw for warmth. Major Charles Preston, the fort's commandant, had sent four couriers to plead for help in Montreal, but no reply had been heard.

For nearly a century, Americans had seen the French in Canada as a blood enemy. New Englanders and New Yorkers especially never forgave the atrocities committed by French raiders and their American Indian confederates at Deerfield, Schenectady, Fort William Henry, and other frontier settlements during the Seven Years' War. Britain's triumph in that war against France and its acquisition of New France in 1763—known in Quebec as "the Conquest"—gladdened American hearts. Many French Canadians left for France. Priests lost the right to collect money to support the church and Catholicism was no longer the established state religion. A small commercial class of English merchants friendly to American traders took root.

As tensions with Britain increased, many Americans—Benjamin Franklin and Samuel Adams among them—considered Canada a natural part of a united North America. The First Continental Congress in October 1774 sent Canadians an open letter, at once welcoming and sinister: "You have been conquered into liberty . . . You are a small people, compared to those who with open arms invite you into fellowship." Canadians faced a choice between having "all the rest of North America your unalterable friends, or your inveterate enemies."

War in Massachusetts, and the American capture of Forts Ticonderoga and Crown Point, brought matters to a head. In Congress, debate raged for weeks. Even General Washington, who had qualms about opening another front in the war, saw the use in capturing Canadian staging grounds so Britain could not use them to amass troops before an inevitable move on New York and New England. Others saw a chance to seize the Canadian granary and fur trade and to delay attacks by Britain's potential American Indian allies. In late June, Congress finally ordered Major General Philip Schuyler, a well-born New Yorker, to launch attacks to prevent Britain from seizing Lake Champlain. He was authorized to "take possession of St. Johns, Montreal, and any other parts of the country" if "practicable" and if the intrusion "will not be disagreeable to the Canadians."

BENJAMIN FRANKLIN, WEARING THE FUR CAP HE OBTAINED IN CANADA. [LOC]

For two months little had gone right in the campaign. Schuyler's Northern Army, as the invasion troops were named, comprised 1,200 ill-trained, ill-equipped, insubordinate troops, many without decent muskets or gunsmiths at hand to fix them.

MAJOR GENERAL PHILIP SCHUYLER, COMMANDER OF AMERICAN TROOPS IN NORTHERN NEW YORK. [LOC]

Alarming reports in late August of British vessels at St. Johns preparing to move onto Lake Champlain forced the Americans into motion. Brigadier General Richard Montgomery set out from Ticonderoga on August 31 with the 1,200 men and four twelve-pounders aboard a schooner, a sloop, and a mismatched group of smaller boats and canoes.

The initial efforts by the invaders were feeble. When moving toward the fort at St. Johns they were ambushed by the Iroquois and British regulars. In another instance, the men were spooked by strange noises and "ran like sheep," in Montgomery's contemptuous phrase. With difficulty and a threat of bayoneting, they were restrained from pushing off in the boats and abandoning their officers on the shoreline. Despite such misfires and misadventures, Montgomery soon had control at St. Johns.

Reinforcements streamed north across Lake Champlain in October, including Connecticut regiments and a New York artillery detachment with siege guns, bringing American strength to 2,700. Gunners built batteries south of the fort and across the Richelieu River to the northeast. After a fifty-three-day siege, with sixty defenders killed or wounded, his food and powder all but gone, Major Charles Preston, the British commander, had finally had enough. He stalled for a day by trying to squeeze concessions from the Americans. Would the honors of war be observed? Could officers keep their baggage? Sidearms? Why not permit the men to sail for England on parole?

At 8:00 a.m. on November 3, Montgomery's men shouldered their muskets in a field south of the fort. A few wore smart uniforms, like the gunners in blue coats with buff facings; more sported the drab outfits of laborers. To the trill and rap of fife and drum, the defeated garrison marched six abreast with colors flying through the gate, some of them mud-caked, their feet bound in rags. First came the 26th Foot in brick-red coats with pale yellow facings;

then the Royal Fusiliers with blue facings; then Royal Artillery troops in dark blue coats and once-white waistcoats, drawing two small guns; and finally sailors in pigtails, American Indians in blankets and feathers, a few kilt-clad Scots, carpenters, cooks, servants, and a gaggle of women and fretful children. On Preston's order the troops shuffled into the waiting flat-bottomed bateaux for the long journey across Champlain to captivity in New England.

More than three quarters of the British regulars in Canada had now been captured or killed, along with virtually all of the trained artillerymen. The booty from St. Johns included seventeen fine brass guns, two brass howitzers, twenty-two iron guns, eight hundred muskets and bayonets, sails, pitch, tar, and precious nails. The cost of the long siege to the American invaders was steep—a hundred combat casualties and another thousand men, including their commander, General Schuyler, sent back to New York with various ailments. But the front door to Canada had swung open, and thousands of additional Continentals stood ready to march through. Montreal beckoned.

The Northern Army plodded northwest from St. Johns toward the St. Lawrence River, through "mud and mire and scarce a spot of dry ground for miles together," a Connecticut chaplain noted. Foul weather and a shortage of boats delayed crossing the river, but on November 9, Montgomery sent an ultimatum: Unless Montreal unlocked its gates, he would destroy the town, leaving eight thousand residents homeless in a Canadian winter. By Sunday, November 12, when Montgomery reached Récollet, in the southwest suburbs, a delegation of frightened Montreal merchants agreed to his surrender terms. Rarely had a fortified town fallen so easily.

But Major General Guy Carleton, the British governor and

commanding general in Canada, slipped away just as Montgomery arrived. He and ninety loyal companions had launched from the wharf in the *Gaspé* and ten smaller boats. The formidable Carleton would lead other men to battle.

One final objective remained before Canada could be considered an American possession, and that lay 144 miles down the St. Lawrence River. "I need not tell you that till Quebec is taken, Canada is unconquered," Montgomery wrote his brother-in-law.

TEN

QUEBEC, CANADA

September–November 1775

With the seizure of Ticonderoga and Crown Point, Benedict Arnold burst into American history, never to leave. After securing both forts in May 1775, wearing a scarlet militia uniform coat with buff facings and big epaulets, he led three dozen men on a brief raid across Lake Champlain into Canada to capture thirteen prisoners and a sloop—the *George*, which he renamed *Enterprise*. In a long letter to the Continental Congress, Arnold was among the first to urge an invasion of Canada via St. Johns, Chambly, and Montreal. A few weeks later, he took the opportunity to convince General Washington that he was the right man to lead a second invasion force directly to Fortress Quebec along a rugged trail used for the past century by American Indians, Jesuit missionaries, and French trappers. His proposed route followed the Kennebec and Chaudière Rivers from the coast of the Eastern Country—still part of Massachusetts, but later to become Maine—to the St. Lawrence valley.

Washington chose to take a chance on him. The commander in chief had contemplated a similar expedition through Canada's back

COLONEL BENEDICT ARNOLD, LEADER OF AN AMERICAN EXPEDITION THROUGH THE MAINE WILDERNESS INTO CANADA, SEEN WITH THE WALLED CITY OF QUEBEC IN THE BACKGROUND. *[LOC]*

door, and this scrappy, enterprising, persuasive fighter seemed worth a gamble. In early September, he gave Arnold a Continental Army colonel's commission and permission to recruit 1,100 "active woodsmen" from the regiments in Cambridge for a mission that was "secret though known to everybody," as one officer noted. "Not a moment's time is to be lost," Washington wrote. "The season will be considerably advanced." He believed "that Quebec will fall into our hands a very easy prey."

After marching forty miles north from Cambridge to Newburyport, Arnold's brigade paraded with flags flying near the Merrimack River and clambered onto eleven small trading boats stinking of fish. By September 22, they had traveled more than one hundred miles up the Maine coast, to a shipyard on the banks of the Kennebec River. Here, on Washington's orders, 220 flat-bottomed bateaux were under construction, with flaring sides, tapered ends, and more than 1,300 paddles, oars, and poles to pull them through shallow water. Not only were the boats extremely heavy, they also leaked from the moment they touched water, requiring constant bailing. With seams opening faster than they could be caulked, casks of dried peas, salt fish, and beef swelled and spoiled; a hundred tons of provisions—the men ate three thousand pounds of food each day—dwindled at an alarming rate as the fleet nosed north. Arnold urged them on with cries of "To Quebec and victory!"

Few military expeditions would be more heroic or more heartbreaking. Terrible storms, sudden heavy snowfalls, the desertion of Arnold's rear battalion, and severe starvation plagued the group.

COLONEL BENEDICT ARNOLD'S TROOPS CARRY FLAT-BOTTOM BOATS CALLED BATEAUX AROUND SHOWHEGAN FALLS IN MAINE AS THEY ADVANCE TOWARD CANADA. [LOC]

Salvation appeared in the form of cattle: At midday on Thursday, November 2, forty miles north of Lac-Mégantic, a small herd of cattle ambled up the riverbank, driven by several French Canadians. Ravenous men ate their fill by an open fire. In the coming days Arnold's troops straggled into Sartigan, filthy, feeble, their clothes torn and their beards matted. Of the 1,080 who had set out from Cambridge in September, about 400 had turned back, been sent home as invalids, or died on the journey.

Ever aggressive, Arnold next resolved to seize Quebec immediately. During the following week, as the men regained health and weight, he hired carpenters and smiths to make scaling ladders, spears, and grappling hooks. Muskets were repaired, canoes purchased. Company by company, the men moved north to Pointe-Levy, three miles up the St. Lawrence from Quebec, where locals welcomed them with a country dance featuring bagpipes, fiddle music, and sips of rum.

But after crossing the great river on November 13 to almost

within cannon range of Quebec's great walls, Arnold learned from his spies that the enemy garrison had grown to nearly 1,900 men—three times the American strength. Arnold prudently ordered his men to pull back to the west to wait for General Montgomery to arrive downriver from Montreal.

Aware that Britain would likely dispatch a robust force in the spring to regain the empire's losses in Canada, both Washington and Schuyler believed that Fortress Quebec must be quickly reduced in the coming weeks, then occupied and fortified over the winter to withstand the anticipated assault. Although more than six tons of gunpowder had been sent to the Northern Army, mostly from South Carolina and New York, shortages persisted of everything from food and winter clothing to money and munitions. Still, with Montgomery and Arnold leading their "famine-proof veterans," victory in the north seemed at hand.

ELEVEN

QUEBEC, CANADA

December 3, 1775–January 1, 1776

On December 3, the sight of canvas sails gliding down the St. Lawrence River brought Colonel Arnold and his troops tromping through snow to the river's edge from the farmhouses where they had found shelter. The brig *Gaspé*, the schooner *Mary*, and several smaller vessels—all seized from the British as they'd tried to flee Montreal two weeks earlier—rounded a point on the north bank, nosing through patches of ice, then dropped their anchors. Cheers echoed through the aspens as a skiff from the little flotilla scraped onto the beach and Brigadier General Richard Montgomery stepped ashore, ready to complete the conquest of Quebec.

Montgomery brought three hundred men, cannons, mortars, and winter clothing confiscated from enemy stocks, including sealskin moccasins, red cloth caps trimmed in fur, captured British

BRIGADIER GENERAL RICHARD MONTGOMERY. [LOC]

uniforms, and full-skirted winter overcoats. Forty more barrels of gunpowder—two tons—would shortly follow. The soldiers now numbered just under one thousand, still about half of what Arnold thought they would need.

On Monday, the Americans rode by sleigh or walked twenty miles to the snow-covered Plains of Abraham. In a long dispatch to General Schuyler, Montgomery concluded that "the works of Quebec are extremely extensive, and very incapable of being defended." Yet laying siege to the town hardly seemed feasible, given the small American numbers and the lack of heavy guns; his biggest cannons were twelve-pounders, compared to several thirty-two-pounders inside the fortress. He "would not wish to see less than ten thousand men ordered here" from the colonies to hold Quebec once the town was captured, since Britain no doubt would send reinforcements in the spring to take it back.

The Americans circled the walled city, Arnold and his men to the north, Montgomery and his to the south. No sooner were they in place than disgruntlement crept into their ranks. Brutal cold and British cannonading proved dispiriting; the huts used for barracks were filthy and infested with lice, bedbugs, and fleas; and the disease smallpox had begun to spread. By Christmas two hundred men had died or deserted.

Montgomery considered several attack strategies and settled on a direct assault. Two columns—led by Montgomery and Arnold—would approach from opposite directions on a stormy night to capture the Lower Town along the St. Lawrence. Two smaller diversionary forces would move toward Cape Diamond and the St. John Gate. If the narrow, heavily defended Mountain Hill Street leading to the Upper Town could not be forced, Montgomery hoped that Major General Carleton would be pressured by civilian merchants to surrender Quebec rather than let the warehouses, dockyards, and shipping be destroyed.

Each American soldier prepared for battle in his own fashion. Many settled their debts and washed their clothes; wood smoke from drying racks perfumed shirts and pants. They finished sharpening pikes and building scaling ladders. "Got all in readiness with our ladders, spears, and so forth, with hearts undaunted," wrote a Rhode Islander who had taken up soldiering "to make a man of himself." Because so many wore scavenged British uniforms, each man was to fasten recognition emblems to his hat: a hemlock sprig and a scrap of paper with "liberty or death" scribbled on it.

As for Montgomery, he assembled a final conference with his officers on Saturday evening, December 30. A vicious storm had begun to blow from the northeast, with heavy snow and frigid winds. Once again, they reviewed the plan: two diversions, then two converging attacks on the Lower Town.

Four a.m. had come and gone when an odd flicker of light to the west caught British captain Malcolm Fraser's watchful eye as he trudged between sentry posts along the fortress ramparts. Fraser squinted through the blowing snow across the Plains of Abraham. Lanterns? Torches? Abruptly two crimson rockets arced into the sky, followed by the dull pop of distant gunfire. Skidding on the slick cobbles, Fraser raced to the Récollet monastery, where his soldiers were sleeping, bellowing, "Turn out! Turn out!" General Carleton met him at the entrance and ordered a general alarm.

Arnold had assembled almost five hundred men with scaling ladders near the St. Charles convent in St. Roch. Upon spotting

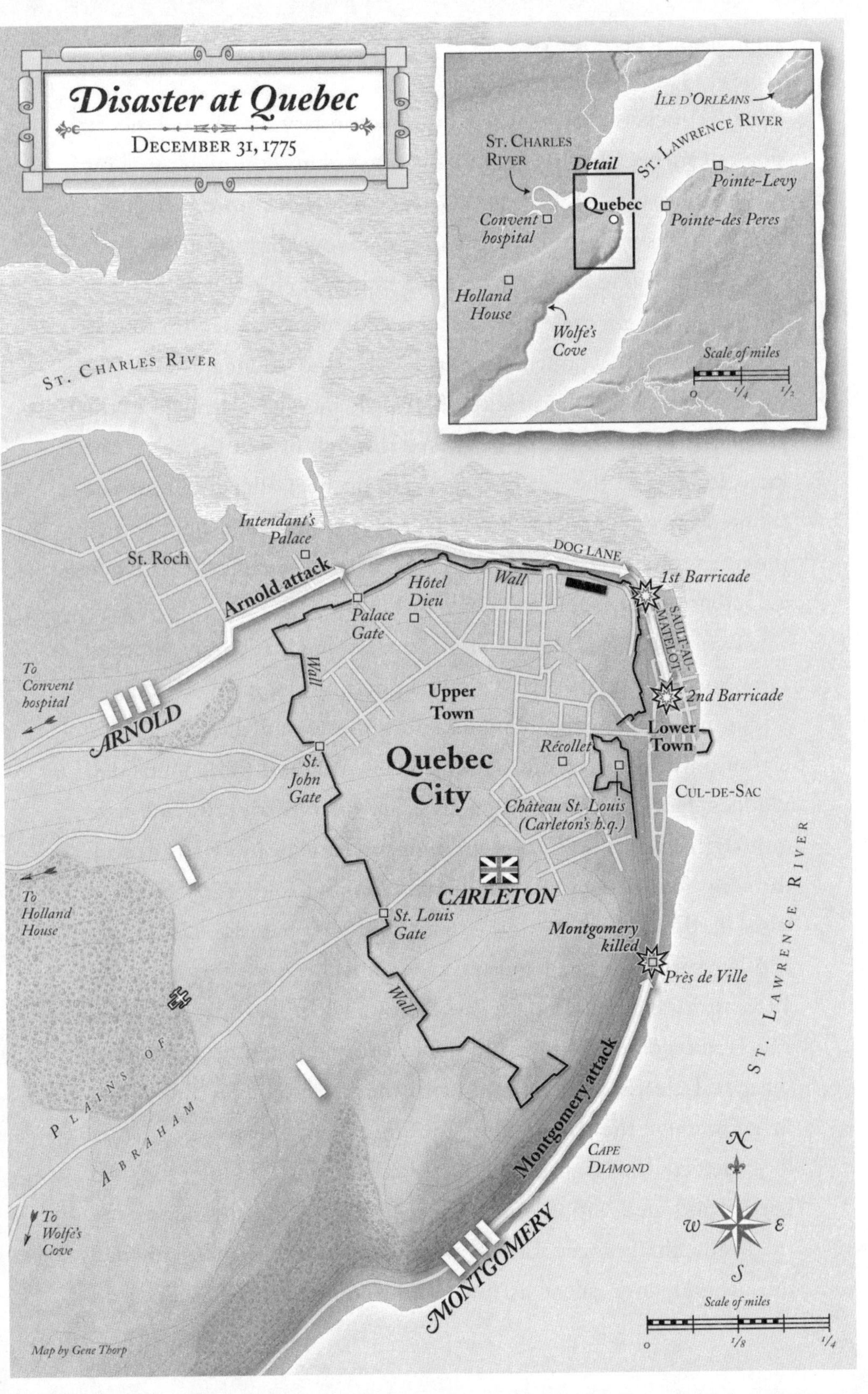
Disaster at Quebec
December 31, 1775
Île d'Orléans
St. Lawrence River
St. Charles River
Detail
Quebec
Pointe-Levy
Pointe-des Peres
Convent hospital
Holland House
Wolfe's Cove
Scale of miles
0
1/4
1/2
St. Charles River
Intendant's Palace
St. Roch
Dog Lane
Arnold attack
1st Barricade
Hôtel Dieu
Wall
Palace Gate
Sault-au-Matelot
To Convent hospital
2nd Barricade
Upper Town
Arnold
Lower Town
Récollet
St. John Gate
Quebec City
Cul-de-Sac
Château St. Louis (Carleton's h.q.)
To Holland House
Carleton
St. Louis Gate
Montgomery killed
Près de Ville
St. Lawrence River
Plains of Abraham
Montgomery attack
Cape Diamond
To Wolfe's Cove
N
W
E
S
Montgomery
Scale of miles
0
1/8
1/4
Map by Gene Thorp

the two rockets that signaled the diversionary attacks on the far side of Quebec, they set off in a snaking column through the snow. As he approached the Palace Gate on Quebec's northern shoulder, Arnold swung into Dog Lane to follow the wall toward the Lower Town. The rampart overhead immediately erupted in muzzle flashes, raking the Americans. Arnold's men hurried on toward a ten-foot-high wooden barrier. He had no sooner ordered his men to prop ladders against the barricade than he crumpled to the ground: A bullet fragment had sliced through his left leg below the knee, lodging in the calf muscle above his heel. Bleeding badly, he shouted encouragement through gritted teeth while hobbling to the rear with help from two men, who carried him the final mile to a doctor's surgery table at a convent hospital.

Two miles southwest, Montgomery led his three hundred New Yorkers along the St. Lawrence shoreline from Wolfe's Cove. Squinting through the blinding snow, they spied the first fortification on this side of the Lower Town—a fifteen-foot, unguarded wooden fence blocking the path. Carpenters with saws and axes quickly hacked a hole large enough for Montgomery to squeeze through, followed by his command staff and soldiers. A hundred yards farther north, near the King's Wharf and the old forges, another barrier loomed and was overcome. Montgomery now saw a two-story blockhouse fifty yards ahead. He crept forward as others clambered behind him. No light or sound could be heard from what was clearly a stronghold, with musket loopholes and closed firing ports on the second floor. An officer sent forward for a closer look detected no sign of enemies. Perhaps this building, too, had been abandoned. Montgomery drew his sword and advanced.

Inside, three dozen British and Canadian militiamen crowded the ground floor, silent as mice, while nine sailors upstairs held lighted matches next to several small cannons packed with grapeshot. When Montgomery and his men were at point-blank range, perhaps no more than twenty yards, the captain gave the command: "Fire!" The ports flew open. Flame spurted from the muzzles and detonations broke the early morning silence.

Grapeshot hit Montgomery in both thighs and, mortally, through the face. He pitched over backward, knees drawn up, the sword flying from his hand. Twelve other bodies would also be found in the snow. The survivors had plunged back, dragging the wounded by their collars.

***THE DEATH OF GENERAL RICHARD MONTGOMERY AT QUEBEC ON DECEMBER 31, 1775.* [LOC]**

Now the American attack came fully unstitched. British reinforcements followed the trail of blood down Dog Lane and rebel soldiers scattered. American guns were wet and misfired again and again. A British nine-pounder convinced even the diehards that the battle was lost. Eyes hollow, faces stained with powder, the Americans tossed their muskets into the street and stepped out with their hands raised in surrender.

TWELVE

BOSTON, MASSACHUSETTS

January–March 1776

The new year brought boredom, sickness, and more misery to British-occupied Boston. "The cold is so intense that the ink freezes in the pen whilst I write by the fireside," a lieutenant wrote to a friend on December 31. General Howe warned London that he had only three weeks of fuel left for his garrison. Firewood had grown so scarce that countless trees had already been reduced to stumps. Selected fences, barns, wharves, sailing vessels, warehouses, and a hundred dilapidated houses had been dismantled and the pulpit and pews from the Old South church were chopped up for kindling.

The winter passed pleasantly enough at Vassall House in Cambridge. Washington's headquarters had good furniture, and a well-stocked pantry. The house had become even livelier in mid-December with the arrival of Martha Washington in a white carriage adorned with the family crest, accompanied by five enslaved people wearing scarlet livery. Lady Washington had never been north of Alexandria, Virginia, but would henceforth share her husband's camp life for half of the war's one hundred months.

Across the American encampment, drums beat each morning at first light, and troops manned the lines in force to repel any surprise attack. After sunrise they marched to prayers. Chaplains attended their souls while sergeants and junior officers worked on their soldiering skills. British artillery peppered the rebel lines every day, to modest effect. Washington, unmistakable in his blue silk sash, often rode out with his spyglass to Prospect and Cobble Hills.

For two months, Washington had struggled, as he told Hancock, to simultaneously "disband one army and recruit another" within musket range of "twenty-odd British regiments." He could only guess how many Americans remained in the Northern Army in Canada, and had yet to hear of Montgomery's catastrophe at Quebec. So desperate was Washington for manpower that he reversed an earlier order prohibiting free Blacks from reenlisting. Roughly five thousand African Americans would eventually serve in the Continental Army, a more racially integrated national force than would exist for nearly two centuries.

After bitter debate, in late December, Congress had directed Washington to evict the enemy from Boston "notwithstanding the town and the property in it may thereby be destroyed."

But how? Nearly two thousand soldiers in his feeble army lacked firearms. Washington asked New England governors to send five thousand militiamen for extended duty, but they arrived with little gunpowder. Close living led to sickness. No malady worried Washington more than what some called the "king of terrors." "Smallpox rages all over the town," he wrote to Hancock.

For now, the camp and the country round about it settled into the rhythms of a winter siege and waited for spring. Most American troops stood idle. "We really are tired of inaction," wrote Stephen Moylan, the army's muster-master general.

Good news, very good news, reached Washington's headquarters on Thursday, January 18, when a bulky, bowlegged man with brilliant gray eyes rode into Cambridge after a two-month absence. Here was young Henry Knox to announce that against stiff odds he had transported, in midwinter by boat and by sled, fifty-eight fine guns more than two hundred miles from Forts Ticonderoga and Crown Point—cannons and mortars, brass and iron. Those guns, momentarily parked twenty miles to the west on a muddy roadside in Framingham, were now his, and he was ready and eager to blow the British out of his hometown.

BOSTON BOOKSELLER HENRY KNOX, A VOLUNTEER IN WASHINGTON'S ARMY, WOULD RISE TO COMMAND ALL CONTINENTAL ARTILLERY. [LOC]

Knox was an unlikely savior. At age eighteen, he had joined the British militia artillery company and learned to fire cannons, although he had lost two fingers in a hunting accident. The bookshop he owned in Boston had been popular before the war with both British officers and well-heeled Bostonians.

Perhaps sensing the inevitable, Henry and his wife, Lucy, had fled Boston in the spring of 1775, and he joined the American camp. Though still a volunteer waiting for his commission from Congress, he'd impressed Washington with the way he shot the army's largest guns with his big, imperfect hands. Many had considered the mission to Ticonderoga a fool's errand, but now Washington had the firepower needed to evict the British.

✦✦✦

Knox was at Washington's elbow at 10:00 a.m. on February 11, a frigid Sunday, when they rode to Roxbury for another look at the lay of the land. After a brief conference with Major General Artemas Ward, commanding the right wing of the Continental Army, the men headed, spyglasses in hand, two miles east to the swampy isthmus that led to Dorchester Heights. The summit of Dorchester Heights offered a panoramic view of Boston, the harbor, and the British garrison at Castle William on an island to the east.

HENRY KNOX, ON HORSEBACK, AND AMERICAN TROOPS USE SLEDS TO TRANSPORT DISASSEMBLED BRITISH CANNONS CAPTURED AT FORT TICONDEROGA BACK TO WASHINGTON'S ARMY NEAR BOSTON. [LOC]

Washington longed for a decisive battle. With ample guns now available, perhaps a solution to the standoff in Boston could be found on this commanding ground south of town, despite the shortage of Continental troops, small arms, and powder. He positioned extra sentries around the heights to ensure that the British did not try to seize the high ground before he did.

The heavy sleds from Framingham began to creep toward Roxbury, along with wagons stacked high with swamp timber.

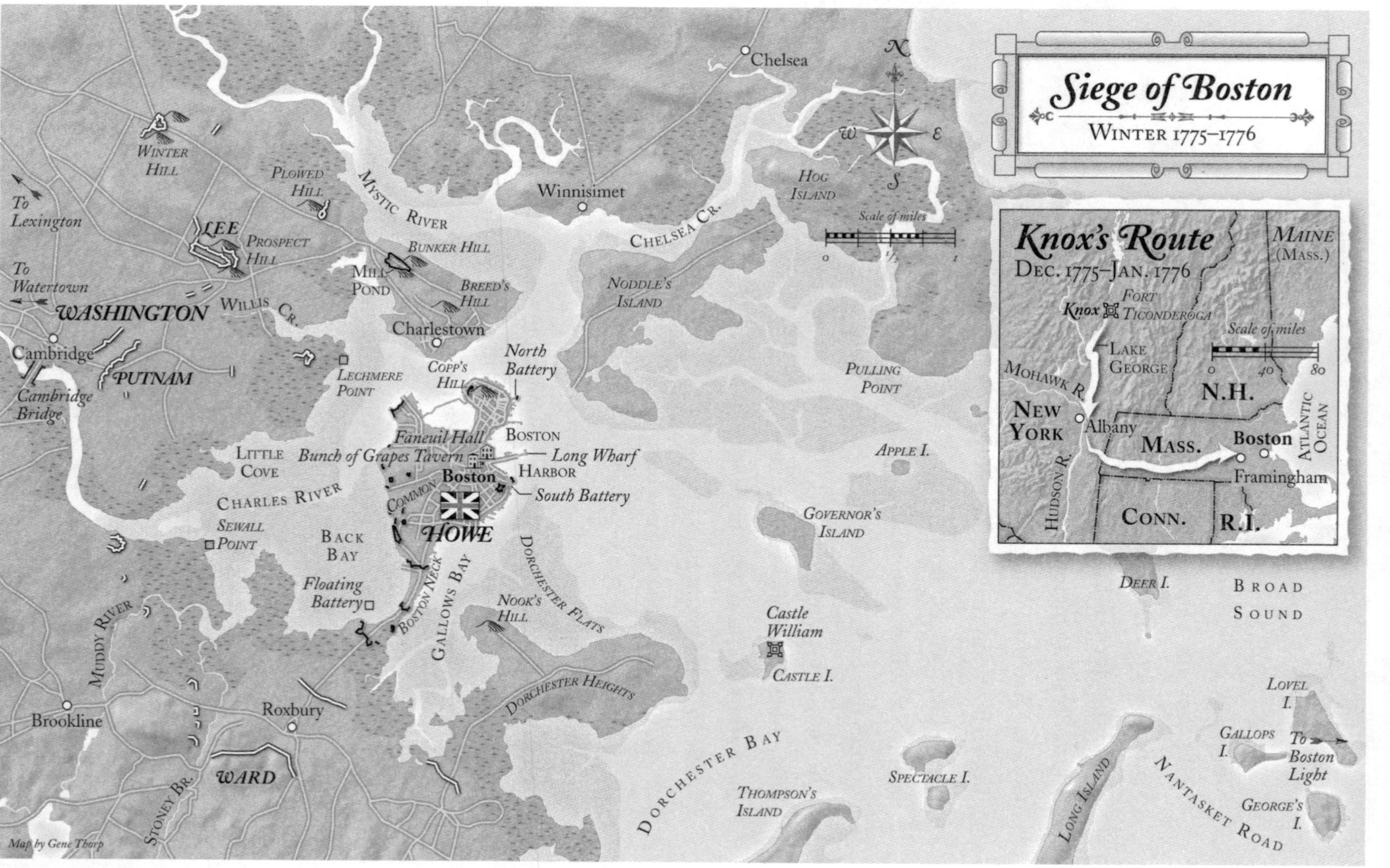
Siege of Boston
Winter 1775–1776
Knox's Route
Dec. 1775–Jan. 1776
Knox
Fort Ticonderoga
Lake George
Mohawk R.
New York
Albany
Hudson R.
N.H.
Maine (Mass.)
Mass.
Boston
Framingham
Atlantic Ocean
Conn.
R.I.
Scale of miles
0
40
80
N
S
E
W
Scale of miles
0
1/2
1
Chelsea
Winnisimet
Chelsea Cr.
Hog Island
Noddle's Island
Pulling Point
Apple I.
Governor's Island
Deer I.
Broad Sound
Castle William
Castle I.
Lovel I.
Gallops I.
To Boston Light
George's I.
Nantasket Road
Long Island
Spectacle I.
Thompson's Island
Dorchester Bay
Dorchester Heights
Dorchester Flats
Nook's Hill
Gallows Bay
Boston Neck
South Battery
Long Wharf
Boston Harbor
North Battery
Copp's Hill
Faneuil Hall
Bunch of Grapes Tavern
Boston
Common
Howe
Back Bay
Floating Battery
Charles River
Little Cove
Sewall Point
Lechmere Point
Charlestown
Breed's Hill
Bunker Hill
Mill Pond
Mystic River
Plowed Hill
Winter Hill
Prospect Hill
Lee
Willis Cr.
Washington
Putnam
Cambridge
Cambridge Bridge
To Lexington
To Watertown
Muddy River
Brookline
Roxbury
Ward
Stoney Br.
Map by Gene Thorp

THIRTEEN

BOSTON, MASSACHUSETTS

March 1776

The seizure of Dorchester Heights was planned for Monday night, March 4, and Washington's headquarters at Vassall House in Cambridge bustled with couriers, officers, and aides-de-camp swaggering in and out. In every redoubt, guns were "to be examined, cleaned, and collected in their proper places"; men without muskets would receive lances. Troops were "positively forbid playing of cards and other games of chance at this time of public distress." Hundreds of axmen began clear-cutting orchards, then sharpening branches and tree trunks for abatis and barricades on the high ground.

With two thousand casualties expected, carts were positioned to wheel the wounded from the battlefield. Barracks on Prospect Hill and at Harvard College became hospital wards. Two dozen regimental surgeons met at Brown's Tavern for their assignments; among them they counted only six sets of amputation instruments, two cases of surgical knives, 859 bandages, twenty-four tourniquets, and "but few medicines."

HARVARD COLLEGE WAS USED AS A HOSPITAL DURING THE AMERICAN CAPTURE OF DORCHESTER HEIGHTS, THE KEY TO FORCING THE BRITISH ARMY OUT OF BOSTON. *[LOC]*

For more than a week, informants had warned General Howe of danger afoot. "Deserters say they intend to . . . bombard the town from Dorchester," Major Stephen Kemble, a British deputy general, noted on February 29. "But as yet no sign of their works." Meandering, fretful conversations about possible intervention led to nothing, and by sunrise on Tuesday, March 5, it was too late. British officers clutching their spyglasses pounded up to the rooftops, mouths agape. "A most astonishing night's work," an engineer told his diary with professional admiration. "Must have employed from 15 to 20,000 men." The rebels, another officer wrote, "raised the forts with an expedition equal to that of the genie belonging to Aladdin's wonderful lamp."

Fire from above could now scour the anchorage, the docks, and the town. Gun ports on the men-of-war flew open and British shore batteries swiveled toward Dorchester. Soon a cannonade unlike any ever known in Boston blistered the hillsides. But most shots failed to reach the American works.

Anticipating a British lunge toward Dorchester, Washington

had organized a counterstrike. Two floating batteries and forty-five bateaux—each capable of carrying eighty men—were positioned up the Charles River. Under General Israel Putnam, four thousand troops in Cambridge stood ready to make an amphibious assault on Boston should Howe's army move toward the heights.

Lookouts were posted on Washington's order, with "the best glasses you can procure" to follow enemy movements. The raising of a flag atop Prospect Hill would launch the counterattack. That signal never came. First, delays in loading British troops and artillery at Long Wharf caused Howe to postpone the Dorchester charge until the morning tide on Wednesday, March 6. But by early Tuesday evening, rain and hail from the south lashed regulars and Continentals alike. Gale winds blew down rail fences and sheds, and drove three British transport ships aground. The tempest persisted into Wednesday morning, churning "so great a surf on the shore where the troops must have landed that it was impossible a boat could live," a British officer recorded. The transports tacked back to Long Wharf, to the immense disappointment of Washington, who had imagined that by Wednesday evening Dorchester's slopes would be plastered with dead redcoats.

MAJOR GENERAL ISRAEL PUTNAM. [LOC]

Convening another war council at Province House, Howe praised "the honor of the troops" in their willingness to fight, then announced the inevitable: The army would abandon Boston immediately. Rebel possession of Dorchester Heights was simply the last straw. The British had less than six weeks of food remaining, including only seventeen days of salt pork and ten days of peas.

"I am justly sensible," Howe told London, "how much more [useful] . . . it would be to His Majesty's service if this army was in a situation to proceed immediately to New York." But food shortages and the danger of meeting a hostile reception required sailing first to the British base at Halifax, Nova Scotia, a two-week voyage to the northeast. Loyalists evacuated from Boston could be deposited there, and Howe also intended to retrain and reorganize his force. He would send home officers impaired with "age and infirmities," promote worthy replacements, adapt uniforms and formations to North American combat, and hone the army's light infantry and amphibious tactics.

By Thursday, March 7, news of the imminent departure had filtered through the ranks. No one was pleased by the prospect of months in Halifax. "Of all the miserable places I ever saw," one captain wrote, "Halifax is the worst."

The British empire would soon possess not a single port on the Atlantic seaboard between Canada and Florida. The ignominy of being evicted from Boston stung every man proud of his uniform.

At 8:00 a.m. on Sunday, March 17, a signal recalled the final British detachment from Bunker Hill. Two officers pulled shut the obstructions at the foot of Long Wharf and climbed into the last boat. Anchors weighed, the fleet glided with great dignity past Castle William and the harbor entrance. Hundreds of rebels could be seen silhouetted along Dorchester Heights, cheering wildly. "We enjoyed the unspeakable satisfaction," wrote the American surgeon James Thacher, "of beholding their whole fleet under sail."

General Washington had not waited for the fleet to disappear over the horizon before claiming his prize. He orchestrated the entry into Boston as meticulously as Howe had organized his exit. The first thousand Continental troops into the town, he decreed, must be smallpox survivors. An informant had told him that the British had "laid several schemes" to infect his army, and so this vanguard—immune as a consequence of having had the disease—would look for signs of British treachery. A flurry of orders forbade looting, or "digging after hidden treasures in Charlestown," or using "the odious epithets of 'Tory,' or any other indecent language, it being ungenerous, unmanly, and unsoldier-like." General Putnam, who had crossed the Charles with several regiments to land at Sewall's Point, now proclaimed the town liberated in the "name of the thirteen united colonies of North America."

After a 333-day siege, Boston once again was a town at peace. "The sun looks brighter," Abigail Adams wrote to John, "the birds sing more melodiously." A Connecticut sergeant reported, "Females opened their doors & windows with decanters of wine in their hands to bid us welcome." Patriots who had remained for nearly a year to protect their shops or houses had "become thin, and their flesh wasted, but yet in good spirits," a selectman reported.

FOURTEEN
QUEBEC, CANADA

April–June 1776

A large crowd gathered along the St. Lawrence at the foot of Montreal's walls late on Monday afternoon, April 29. They watched a skiff work its way across from the south bank. When the boat drew close, a military guard presented arms, and Brigadier General Benedict Arnold stepped forward with a pronounced limp to welcome the burly old man with wispy gray hair now visible in the bow. Cannons crashed out a salute from the stone ramparts. Wind tore dirty smoke from the muzzles after each round and carried it downstream. The Canada campaign was saved, at least for the moment: Benjamin Franklin had arrived.

THE WALLED CITY OF MONTREAL. *[LOC]*

Franklin followed the general slowly down the Rue Notre-Dame to Arnold's headquarters. Inside, a crowd of local worthies strained for a glimpse of the celebrated Dr. Franklin. After a meal, Arnold led his guest a hundred yards down Notre-Dame to what was described as "the best built and perhaps the best furnished house in town," owned by a merchant prince. Here, Franklin at last tumbled into the first real bed he had seen in weeks. Important work lay ahead, beginning tomorrow. General Washington himself had recently warned that if Britain managed to keep Canada, the American rebellion "at best will be doubtful, hazardous, and bloody." But first, the seventy-year-old Dr. Franklin needed sleep.

This mission to Canada was only the latest service Franklin had rendered his country since returning from London the previous spring. He had been elected to Congress and appointed postmaster general. But it was as a diplomat that he was invaluable. And it was as a diplomat that Congress had dispatched him to Montreal. Under nineteen paragraphs of instructions signed by John Hancock, Franklin's task was nothing less than to restore Canadian faith in America's ideals, innocence, and military commitment after the failure at Fortress Quebec.

What Franklin soon learned was that morale and discipline had collapsed in the invading American army. Soldiers stole horses and food and ransacked Canadian farms. Desertion was rampant. Worse yet, General David Wooster—the arrogant commander of the American forces still besieging Quebec—had alienated many Canadians by arresting priests and loyalists, closing Catholic churches, meddling with the fur trade, and telling Montreal citizens, "I regard the whole of you as enemies and rascals."

Appalled by Arnold's sorry tale, Franklin and his colleagues took another day for further inquiry and reflection. Clearly, they were months too late in coming to Canada. Dithering by Congress had undermined the American venture, perhaps fatally. They were impressed with Arnold, but Arnold had been undermined by Wooster, by bad behavior in the ranks, and by lack of support from the Congress in Philadelphia.

In early May, a new commander arrived to take over at Quebec. Major General John Thomas found his new command in shambles. Of the thousand Americans fit for duty, three hundred refused to fight since their enlistments had recently expired. Another two hundred had just received smallpox inoculations, against orders, and would be quarantined for weeks. The remainder held a perimeter looping more than twenty miles around the city. There was little food and less powder. "I find there is expected from me more than I think I shall be able to [deliver] unless things were in better order," Thomas had written to his wife, Hannah.

Thomas was not aware that the British reinforcements had arrived and were working their way upstream on the St. Lawrence toward Quebec. He did know that the six thousand American reinforcements remained mostly in the Hudson Valley or along Lake Champlain. After several futile attempts to break Quebec's defenses, including attempting to direct a burning ship into the British fleet, Thomas knew he would be forced to abandon the siege. The Northern Army began to melt into the trees. Most eventually reached Lake Champlain. Some, immobilized by smallpox, fell into enemy hands.

The bad news flew swiftly to Montreal. Franklin wrote a final letter to Congress on Friday, May 10: "We are afraid it will not be in our power to render our country any further services in this colony."

The next morning at 8:00 a.m., Franklin bolted south after some difficulty in finding a carriage to rent. It was a difficult three-week journey back to Philadelphia for the ailing statesman.

✦✦✦

General Carleton had reined in his pursuit of the retreating Americans to await the arrival of more regiments from England, but few doubted that the British would soon advance in full force. Food shortages in the American ranks had grown so dire that some troops were put on half rations. And they were soldiers deprived of their leader when General Thomas abruptly died of smallpox. The new commander, General John Sullivan, was unable to reverse the Continentals' fortunes. Relying on misinformation from spies, he sent Brigadier General William Thompson and two thousand of his most able men across the St. Lawrence River at dawn on June 8 to attack the strategic British fort at Trois-Rivières. Confronted by General John Burgoyne with several thousand regulars and British artillery, the Americans faltered and fell back. Pursued by the British, the troops were chased into a swamp, where they were "devoured by mosquitoes of a monstrous size and innumerable numbers," a young captain later recalled. "Nature perhaps never formed a place better calculated for the destruction of an army," a survivor wrote. "The mantle of heaven was our only covering," another added. "No fire, and bad water our only food."

General Thompson hid in the marsh that night and the following day before surrendering. "Generals Carleton and Burgoyne were both there, who treated us very politely," according to an officer captured

MAJOR GENERAL GUY CARLETON, THE BRITISH GOVERNOR OF CANADA. *[LOC]*

with him. "They ordered us refreshments immediately. Indeed, General Burgoyne served us himself."

American casualties totaled about 400, compared to 17 for the British. Carleton reported capturing 244 Americans, including 18 officers. "Upwards of fifty" American bodies were found at Trois-Rivières and in the swamps. Others simply vanished.

MAJOR GENERAL JOHN BURGOYNE HELPED DRIVE AMERICAN FORCES OUT OF CANADA. [LOC]

FIFTEEN

ST. JOHNS, CANADA

June 1776

There was one more fight to come. Early on Friday, June 14, General Carleton boarded a transport at Trois-Rivières and ordered his troops westward to crush the American invaders for good. Ten thousand regulars, Canadians, and American Indians crowded onto more than sixty vessels or marched along the shoreline. Carleton had concocted a clever plan: Burgoyne would disembark with four thousand men to overrun the rebel camp at Sorel, then angle south along the Richelieu River toward Chambly and St. Johns, careful not to chase the Americans too energetically. Carleton would sail another fifty miles up the St. Lawrence with the rest of the army to La Prairie, across from Montreal, then lunge cross-country fifteen miles to St. Johns, cutting off the American retreat.

General Sullivan had no plan, clever or otherwise. On Thursday night, his war council had convened at Sorel to remind him of the many reasons to flee Canada immediately. Sorel was vulnerable to attack from both the right flank—defended by only a stand of aspen saplings—and from the rear. By one tally, of eight thousand

Continentals north of the border, more than three thousand were sick, mostly with smallpox, which was killing thirty men a day. Measles, dysentery, and other afflictions were also taking a toll. Of the twelve tons of salt pork and flour needed to feed the army every day, only a fraction had arrived from New York.

Some colonels were uncertain where parts of their regiments could be found, and some regiments had "not a single man fit for duty," as Sullivan himself conceded. Forty officers had asked to resign their commissions; others simply walked south, in company with enlisted deserters. Instructions from Congress to "contest every foot of the ground" were impossible to follow. If the army was trapped at the mouth of the Richelieu, Sullivan's senior officers told him, he "alone must answer for it." After a long, tense pause, Sullivan agreed to withdraw to Chambly, fifty miles upstream. Hoisting guns, tents, and the infirm into wagons and rivercraft, the garrison abandoned Sorel at 10:00 a.m. on Friday, every man stealing glances over his shoulder.

No one had been more insistent on retreat than Arnold, who several days earlier had traveled from Montreal to inspect the flimsy defenses at Chambly and St. Johns. All hope for luring Canadians to the American cause was now gone, he wrote to Sullivan. "Let us quit them & secure our own country before it is too late. There will be more honor in making a safe retreat than hazarding a battle," he urged. "I am content to be the last man who quits this country, and fall so that my country rise. But let us not fall together."

At 7:00 p.m. on Saturday, Arnold and three hundred Continentals pushed away from Montreal in eleven bateaux. The town had served as the capital of American Canada for six months, but with British troops reportedly only a dozen miles distant, it would be abandoned without a fight. Across the St. Lawrence, Arnold torched his boats, then led his men through mud "half a leg deep" to La Prairie and on toward St. Johns, burning bridges and felling trees across the road behind them as they fled.

Three other corps—two British and one American—were now

AN OVERVIEW OF FORT ST. JOHNS FROM ACROSS THE RICHELIEU RIVER. [LOC]

heading toward the same destination: St Johns. On Sunday, June 16, Carleton's army reached Varennes, on the right bank, then turned southeast toward St. Johns, more than a day behind Arnold. Burgoyne advanced south along the Richelieu. A twenty-mile march to St. Denis on June 15 left his brigade so weak from the summer heat and scarce provisions that he was forced to rest for a day before resuming the march at midnight. On Monday, June 17, the anniversary of the Battle of Bunker Hill, the regulars finally reached Chambly to find the fort and sawmill in flames, and the rebels gone, again. "We began our chase with might & main," Burgoyne's aide wrote, "but the nimble-heel'd rebels had made too much way for us."

On Monday night, still a day ahead of their pursuers, the Americans staggered into St. Johns to be reunited with Arnold's band from Montreal. On Tuesday morning, a war council agreed to abandon St. Johns for Île aux Noix, a small island twelve miles south, near the mouth of Lake Champlain. Thousands of American soldiers in fifteen regiments now jammed this two-hundred-acre malarial hell, perhaps half of them suffering from smallpox or dysentery or some other malady. Day by day, twenty to sixty more fell ill in each regiment. For want of tents, most of the sick lay uncovered on the marshy ground. Two burial pits were dug, one for New England and New York troops bivouacked on the eastern half of the island, the other for New Jersey and Pennsylvania regiments to the west.

Sullivan seemed stupefied by the misery he commanded. Finally, pressed by his subordinates, he consented to an evacuation. "I find myself under an absolute necessity of quitting this island for a place more healthy," he wrote General Washington on June 24. "Otherwise the army will never be able to return."

The hundred-mile procession south from the river and across

the lake began, with Sullivan leading the boats and 1,200 Continentals marching along the shore.

So ended a botched campaign of liberation. It had been foiled by miscalculation and bad luck, starting with delays the previous summer in marching north and in capturing St. Johns. Carleton's narrow escape from Montreal, the disastrous attack at Fortress Quebec, and smallpox all contributed to the American failure. American losses would forever remain imprecise. Since the previous fall, at least twelve thousand troops had marched into Canada, and probably fewer than nine thousand marched back.

Yet even in the summer of 1776, thin silver linings could be glimpsed. The failure to capture Quebec in December prevented having a large occupying army trapped within the walls by enemy reinforcements in the spring. British plans for a thrust into New York were disrupted momentarily by their loss at Boston and retreat to Halifax to regroup, and some combat strength had been diverted from Howe's main force farther south.

SIXTEEN

NEW YORK, NEW YORK

June–September 1776

But New York was still much on the minds of the British. The town had been changed by war. By early summer, more than twelve thousand American soldiers filled tent camps. Hardly a shot had been fired in anger around New York, but perhaps half or more of the twenty-five thousand residents had fled their homes in fear of bloody things to come.

Since February, soldiers and civilians had worked shoulder to shoulder with picks, shovels, and axes to fortify the town. Each morning, fife and drum summoned work crews from every social class, including leather-aproned tradesmen and gentlemen with blistered hands. Enslaved people delivered by their masters worked every day, whites every other day. Sparks flew night and day as smiths made musket barrels, bayonets, and ramrods.

Rebel cannons and gunmen had forced British governor William Tryon aboard the *Duchess of Gordon* to move out of range outside the Narrows, along with *Asia*, *Phoenix*, *Mercury*, *Lively*, and several transports. Rebels used hatchets to chop holes in loyalist

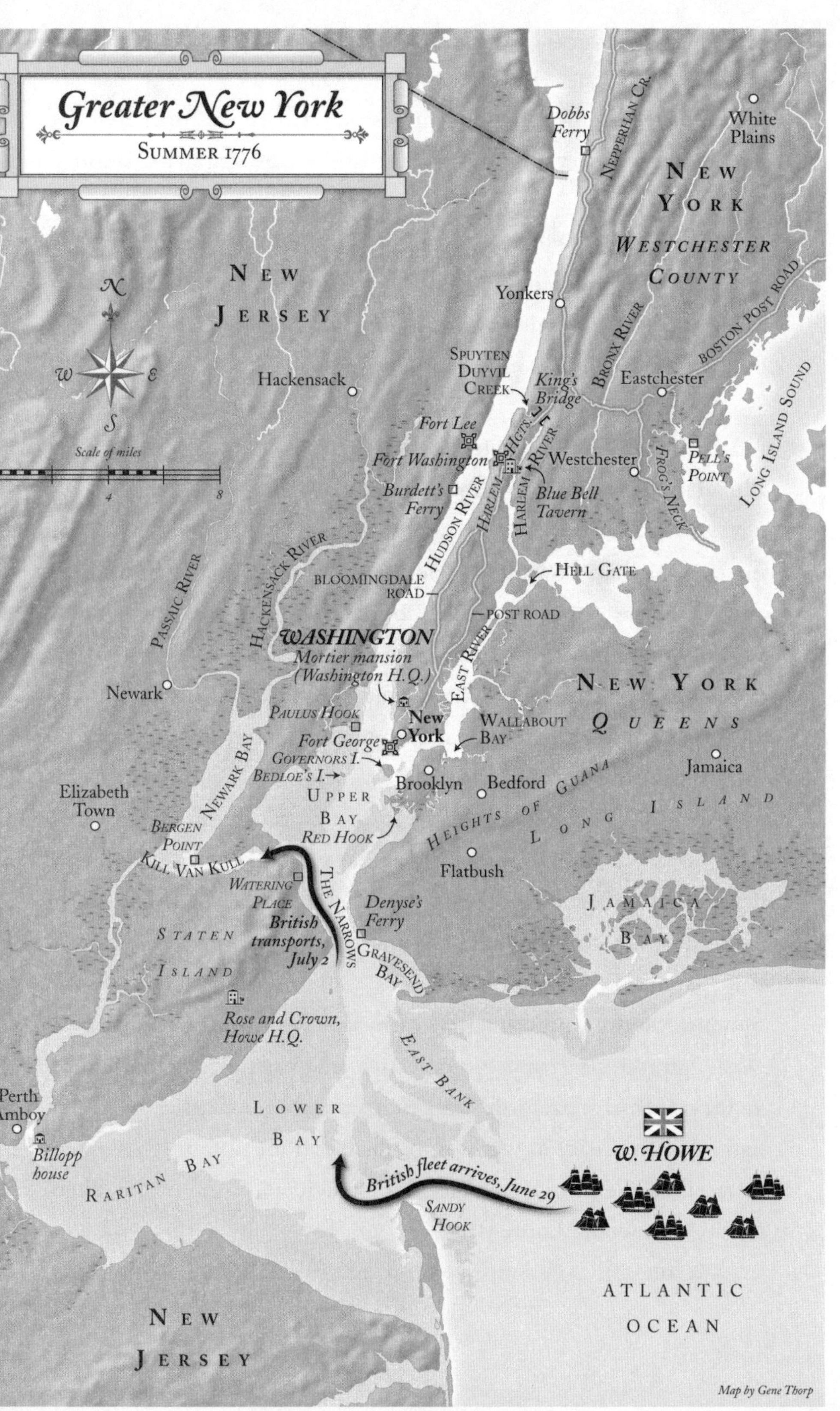

Greater New York
Summer 1776
Scale of miles
4
8
N
W
E
S
New Jersey
New York
Westchester County
Dobbs Ferry
Nepperhan Cr.
White Plains
Yonkers
Boston Post Road
Bronx River
Spuyten Duyvil Creek
King's Bridge
Eastchester
Long Island Sound
Hackensack
Fort Lee
Fort Washington
Hgts.
Harlem River
Westchester
Pell's Point
Frog's Neck
Burdett's Ferry
Hudson River
Harlem
Blue Bell Tavern
Hackensack River
Passaic River
Hell Gate
Bloomingdale Road
Post Road
Washington
Mortier mansion (Washington H.Q.)
East River
New York
Queens
Newark
Paulus Hook
New York
Wallabout Bay
Fort George
Governors I.
Bedloe's I.
Newark Bay
Jamaica
Elizabeth Town
Upper Bay
Brooklyn
Bedford
Heights of Guana
Long Island
Bergen Point
Red Hook
Kill Van Kull
Watering Place
The Narrows
Flatbush
Denyse's Ferry
British transports, July 2
Staten Island
Gravesend Bay
Jamaica Bay
Rose and Crown, Howe H.Q.
East Bank
Perth Amboy
Lower Bay
Billopp house
Raritan Bay
W. Howe
British fleet arrives, June 29
Sandy Hook
Atlantic Ocean
New Jersey
Map by Gene Thorp

boats suspected of smuggling provisions to British crews. Two of the governor's servants were nabbed while bringing his laundry ashore for washing.

That General Howe was sailing south from Halifax, perhaps soon, no one doubted. New York was considered the least disloyal of the thirteen colonies, and those in favor of the Crown lay low and waited for their hour to come round.

On Thursday, June 6, His Excellency General Washington returned to New York after more than a two-week absence in Philadelphia. There he had passed his days discussing grand strategy with Congress. Always careful to pay respect to his political masters, he had consulted delegates individually, in committee, and with the entire assembled body in the Pennsylvania State House. The news from Canada was disquieting, of course. Also, intelligence had reached them that confirmed reports of Britain hiring thousands of German mercenaries to fight in America during the summer.

All in all, Washington had reason to consider his trip to Philadelphia a success. Congress had made clear its determination to defend New York to the death; John Adams described the city as "a kind of key to the whole continent," and Washington agreed it was "a post of infinite importance." Congress also seemed to be moving toward a proclamation of independence. That would give Washington a clear strategic objective, an American definition of victory: formal separation from Britain and the creation of a new nation. Such clarity in war was invaluable. If the country was asked to sacrifice, the purpose would now be evident. If men were asked to die, they would know why.

Washington still longed for a decisive battle. Bleeding the

enemy in New York would dampen support for the war in Britain while emboldening France and other potential American allies. But where to find favorable ground here? Britain's maritime mobility allowed Howe to keep the initiative, landing where and when he chose. Washington also knew that New York's defenses still lacked depth.

On Tuesday, June 18, Washington rode to the Queen's Head Tavern, a former warehouse at Pearl and Broad Streets. His staff and regimental commanders joined him in the Long Room, the town's most spacious public hall, for a banquet arranged by the New York Convention—the provincial congress—in gratitude for defense of the colony. Accompanied by fife and drum, the officers belted out campaign songs. Thirty-one toasts were raised, starting with the Continental Congress and the American army. The final toast was drunk to "civil and religious liberty to all mankind"—all mankind, that is, except Tories.

Of roughly 3.2 million Americans alive from 1775 to 1783, 513,000 demonstrated loyalty by supporting the British cause, fighting with one of two hundred loyalist units, or eventually going into exile. Loyalists often had shallow roots in America; many were recent immigrants rather than native born. Others had ties that bound them to the mother country, as merchants trading with London or Glasgow. Anglican churchgoers tended toward loyalism where they were a minority, as in New England, but not where they were dominant, as in South Carolina. (All Anglican clerics were ordained in Britain and swore allegiance to the king.) Yet with each passing month, loyalist weaknesses became more evident, including the absence of national leaders and an inability to match the rebels in organization, propaganda, or emotional pitch. By the summer of

1776, it had become clear that only massive British support could prop up the loyalist cause.

New York would now become the central battleground, politically and militarily. Determined to purge "Tory Town" of residual loyalists, radical mobs had rampaged through the city breaking windows, stealing livestock, and smashing a loyalist printing press before carrying off the blocks of type to melt into bullets.

For several days, British deserters had warned that the fleet from Halifax was expected hourly. But it still came as a shock at 9:00 a.m. on June 29 when lookouts watching the sea from a Staten Island hilltop hoisted three red-and-white-striped flags, the signal for an approaching fleet of at least twenty ships.

Howe had slipped unnoticed into the Lower Bay four days earlier with a small naval vanguard, and while awaiting the rest of the fleet he spent several days examining the American coastline with his spyglass and questioning Governor Tryon and other loyalists about Washington's troop strength, fortifications, and river defenses. He had intended to land his force promptly at Gravesend Bay on the southwestern rim of Long Island, but reports that rebels infested the ridgeline above the landing beaches caused him to reconsider. Being drawn prematurely into battle would be a mistake; he intended to wait for the arrival—soon, he hoped—of the British and German reinforcements now crossing the Atlantic with the armada commanded by Admiral Lord Richard Howe, his brother. He also expected to be joined before long by General Henry Clinton with his force, although precisely what had happened to them was unclear to General Howe.

The assembly of these legions in New York would give him more than thirty thousand soldiers and an immense fleet, the greatest military force Britain had ever dispatched. Simply the sight of this army would no doubt intimidate the enemy and draw thousands of loyalists back to the Union Jack. "But I am still of opinion," Howe wrote Lord George Germain, the American secretary in King George's cabinet, "that peace will not be restored in America until the rebel army is defeated."

At 8:00 a.m. on Tuesday, July 2, the first three men-of-war—*Phoenix*, *Rose*, and *Greyhound*—eased from the Lower Bay through the Narrows, carefully skirting the East Bank sandbar that made this channel so treacherous. A few random shots from rebel riflemen whizzed above the masts or into the water. Lumbering transports followed toward Kill van Kull, along the upper edge of Staten Island, where Howe knew he would find spring water, summer produce, and citizens loyal to the Crown.

They were welcomed by gleeful loyalists and fugitive enslaved people who offered to serve as guides, teamsters, orderlies, and harbor pilots; more than five hundred Staten Islanders, nearly all

BELLOPP, HOWE'S HEADQUARTERS ON STATEN ISLAND [NYPL]

of the adult male population, would swear allegiance in oaths administered by Governor Tryon. Grenadiers and light infantrymen set up an encampment around a lush oasis called the Watering Place. White tents sprouted in neat rows, and sergeants doled out a generous rum ration. "We are in the most beautiful island that nature could form or art improve," Major Charles Stuart cheerfully wrote to his father. "We have everything we want." The British Army had reclaimed the first corner of New York for the empire.

Washington received accurate intelligence on the new arrivals on Staten Island and their activities. A cascade of orders was issued in the commanding general's name. Fire rafts were built. Small craft, including rowboats, would assemble at docks along the Hudson River. Troops should rehearse moving from their camps to their fighting posts by routes that "are least exposed" to naval gunfire.

Some American commanders favored an immediate attack on Staten Island. But Washington was beginning to understand the merits of strategic defense—outlasting the enemy's will to wage war. Personally aggressive, convinced of the need to keep the British off-balance, he would watch for chances to turn on his foe with great violence. But he also had begun to grasp the agility provided Howe by his navy. As he subsequently wrote to Hancock, "The amazing advantage the enemy derive from their ships and the command of the water keeps us in a state of constant perplexity and the most anxious conjecture."

And, in this unsettled hour, Washington offered his men a glimpse inside his heart:

The time is now near at hand which must probably determine whether Americans are to be freemen or slaves . . . The fate of unborn millions will now depend, under God, on the courage and conduct of this army . . . Let us therefore animate and encourage each other, and show the whole world, that a freeman contending for liberty on his own ground is superior to any slavish mercenary on earth.

SEVENTEEN

CHARLESTON, SOUTH CAROLINA

June 1776

Just as General Howe was unaware of General Clinton's whereabouts, General Clinton was unclear about General Howe's orders. For weeks he had waited on the coast of North Carolina for reinforcements expected from Britain and a response from Howe to his suggestion that they abandon the South in favor of a rendezvous in New York. He felt that no pinprick attacks in the Carolinas were likely to gain hearts and subdue minds. But after four months of silence from Howe, a dispatch finally received from Halifax brought little coherent guidance from the commander in chief. Howe wrote that he intended to make for New York, though he disclosed no timetable and implied no urgency in Clinton's return north. He did mention that Charleston was "an object of importance to His Majesty's service." When the reinforcements finally arrived with a Royal Navy squadron, Clinton shrugged and headed for South Carolina.

Charleston claimed to be the "London of the Low Country," the richest, most sophisticated town in North America's richest colony. By the early summer of 1776, the town had grown to twelve thousand residents—half white and free, half neither. Every coin of Charleston's affluence derived from slavery, from farmhands sold on the Custom House auction block and the ships packed with shackled Gambians and Angolans at Fitzsimmons' Wharf.

MAJOR GENERAL HENRY CLINTON.

Charleston had long been the most heavily fortified city in America. The town sat on a peninsula formed by the meeting of two rivers, the Ashley and the Cooper, which provided natural moats on either flank. Millions of bricks had been laid in defensive works since the early eighteenth century, all reinforced with tabby, a mortar made from crushed oyster shells, lime, sand, ash, and water; a brick "wharf wall" extended for half a mile along the waterfront. In the past year, rumors of a British southern expedition, and the obliteration of coastal towns like Falmouth and Norfolk, had inspired more defenses, mostly constructed by gangs of enslaved people. Warehouses on the wharves were leveled for better fields of fire. Heavy cannons were mounted along South Bay, East Bay, and James Island. A stout fort made of palm logs and sand on Sullivan's Island protected the entrance to Charleston harbor.

ATTACK ON SULLIVAN'S ISLAND.

THE BRITISH FLEET AT CHARLESTON, SOUTH CAROLINA, AFTER THE FAILED ATTACK ON FORT SULLIVAN. [LOC]

Fifty vessels flying the king's colors abruptly filled the anchorage off Charleston in early June. Together they brandished nearly three hundred guns and bore 2,500 soldiers and marines, plus a couple thousand seamen. Clinton and the squadron's naval commander, Commodore Sir Peter Parker, were joined by three floating governors, each driven by rebels from his colony: Josiah Martin of North Carolina, William Campbell of South Carolina, and James Wright of Georgia.

MAJOR GENERAL CHARLES LEE COMMANDED CONTINENTAL ARMY FORCES IN SOUTH CAROLINA. [LOC]

On Saturday, June 8, Major General Charles Lee rode into Charleston with a pack of yapping dogs at his heels and two thousand Continental soldiers from Virginia and North Carolina close behind. Lee was sent by Congress as commander of the newly created Southern Department in hopes of saving Charleston from British attack. His tactical and engineering expertise had proved valuable during the siege of Boston; although no more flamboyant figure ever served the American cause in uniform, Lee had become Washington's most senior lieutenant.

No sooner had Lee dismounted than he was squinting at those sails, fifty sets of them, in Five-Fathom Hole and the adjacent anchorages. With the help of accurate intelligence, including intercepted dispatches from Lord Germain, he had no doubt that General Clinton and his comrades intended to bombard, if not destroy, Charleston. To save the town, the colony, and perhaps the South, Lee had 6,500 troops.

Nothing worried Lee more than the vulnerability of Fort Sullivan. He ordered construction of screens, low walls, and an escape bridge built of empty casks across the Cove, an inlet that separated the island from the mainland. "Sir, when those ships come to lay alongside of your fort," he warned militia colonel William Moultrie, in command at Fort Sullivan, "they will knock it down in half an hour."

If the Americans faced mortal peril in Charleston, the British encountered their own hazards. Getting the ships across the sandbar protecting the harbor and into position was difficult enough, requiring calm seas and precise navigation. As Commodore Parker struggled with his ships, five hundred regulars landed on the northeast shoulder of the nearby Long Island, pitching camp and ferrying supplies ashore through the thundering surf. This, Clinton had concluded, was the ideal place from which to stage his attack on Sullivan's Island, just a short distance across Breach Inlet. Once the rebel defenses at Fort Sullivan were overrun, Charleston would be exposed to assault.

On June 14, Generals Clinton and Charles Cornwallis joined the Long Island camp, followed the next day by soldiers from five troop transport ships. Three more days would be needed, until nightfall on June 18, to land nearly three thousand men with ten guns through squalls and a high sea. And then, calamity. A closer inspection of Breach Inlet revealed a channel that even at low tide was a hundred yards wide and seven feet deep, not the eighteen inches Clinton expected. Officers waded up to their nostrils, searching for a shallow ford that did not exist. To his "unspeakable mortification and disappointment," he sent word to Commodore Parker on the *Bristol*: The army could do little more than conduct a demonstration against Sullivan's Island in hopes of distracting rebel defenders. No landing on the mainland was feasible because of impenetrable swamps, and while the inlet was too deep to wade, it was too shallow for any man-of-war to provide gunfire support.

If astonished and dismayed by this news, Parker was reluctant to concede defeat. The honor of the Royal Navy was at stake, even if the army had been neutralized. He believed that the rebels would crumple under a bombardment unlike anything ever imagined in these parts. No doubt Clinton was correct that there was no time to lose: British navy crews had lived on two-thirds rations for a month and had not eaten fresh meat since North Carolina. Some sailors were already too weak to man their battle stations.

Confusion between the army and navy grew day by day, aggravated by the lack of personal contact between commanders. Neither Clinton nor Parker was certain of the other's intentions.

On Friday morning, June 28, Colonel Moultrie rode to the north end of Sullivan's Island to inspect Colonel William Thomson's defenses at Breach Inlet. As his horse trotted up to the inlet at nine thirty, Moultrie spied a small flotilla of boats carrying redcoats down Hamlin Creek, between the western shore of Long Island and the mainland. No sooner had he asked Thomson his opinion of

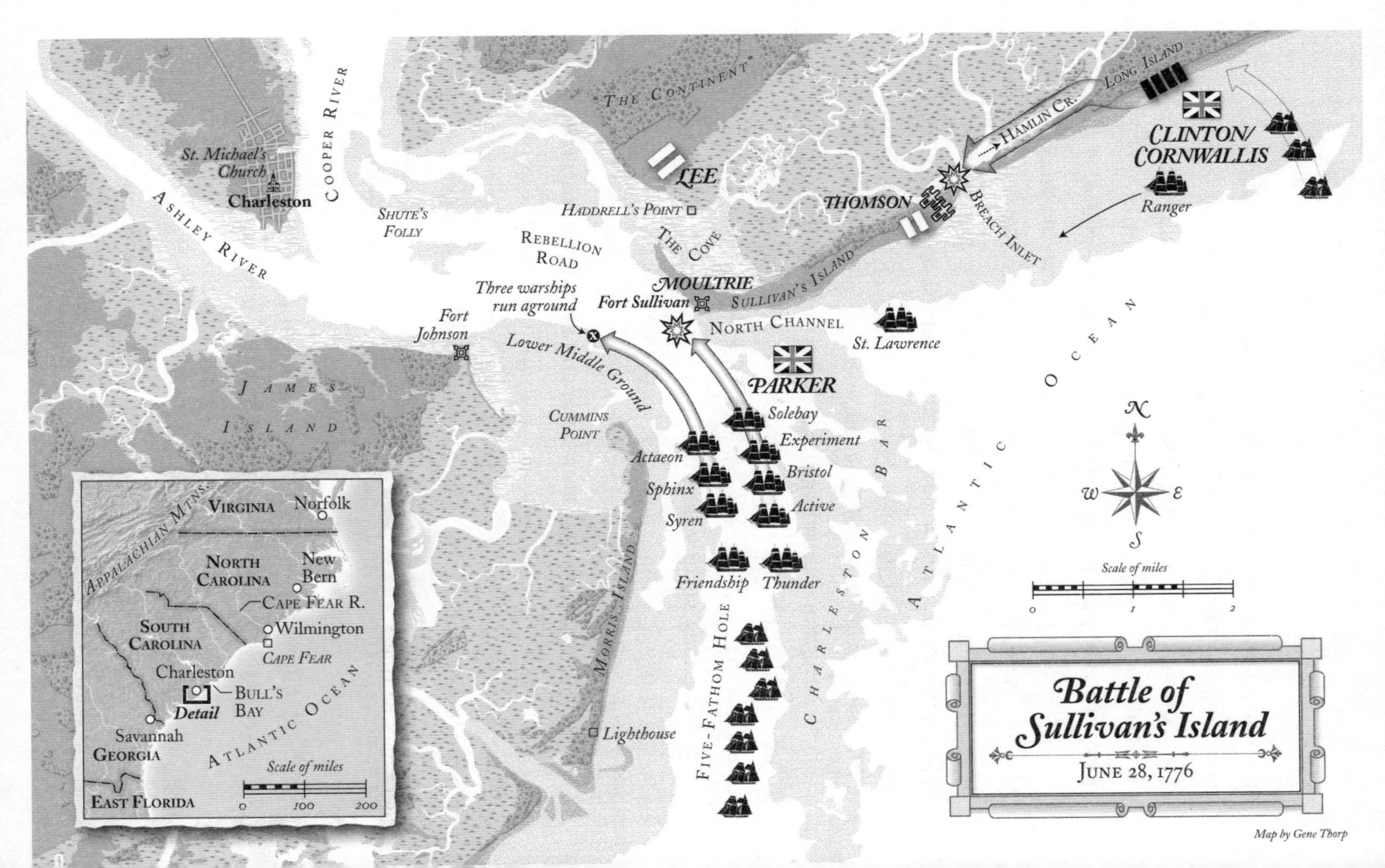
Battle of Sullivan's Island
June 28, 1776
St. Michael's Church
Charleston
Cooper River
Ashley River
Shute's Folly
"The Continent"
Lee
Haddrell's Point
Rebellion Road
The Cove
Hamlin Cr.
Long Island
Clinton/ Cornwallis
Thomson
Breach Inlet
Ranger
Moultrie
Fort Sullivan
Sullivan's Island
Three warships run aground
Fort Johnson
North Channel
St. Lawrence
Lower Middle Ground
Parker
James Island
Cummins Point
Solebay
Experiment
Actaeon
Bristol
Sphinx
Active
Syren
Friendship
Thunder
Morris Island
Five-Fathom Hole
Charleston Bar
Lighthouse
Atlantic Ocean
N
W
E
S
Scale of miles
0
1
2
Virginia
Norfolk
Appalachian Mtns.
North Carolina
New Bern
Cape Fear R.
South Carolina
Wilmington
Cape Fear
Charleston
Bull's Bay
Detail
Savannah
Georgia
Atlantic Ocean
Scale of miles
0
100
200
East Florida
Map by Gene Thorp

this apparition than a shrill cry from a lookout in the dunes warned that British men-of-war in Five-Fathom Hole had loosened their topsails and were inbound on the rising tide. Moultrie yanked his mount around and pounded the three miles back to Fort Sullivan, shouting for his drummer to beat the long roll, summoning the garrison to their battle posts.

Under Commodore Parker's battle plan, four frigates were to deliver the main bombardment against Fort Sullivan. As instructed, the men-of-war glided into position at precise points opposite the fort's long wall and the east and west bastions. Sailors bounded across the decks fixing the guns into position, then opened fire. The weight of metal from each round was fearsome. Balls flew in black flocks across the beach, smacking the bastions with enough thudding violence to make the walls tremble.

Lee galloped from Charleston to Haddrell's Point, gaping offshore at "the most furious fire I ever saw or heard." He sent an aide by canoe to tell Moultrie that should he run out of ammunition, "spike your guns and retreat with all order possible."

Moultrie had no intention of spiking his guns, retreating, or losing the battle. The fort's walls, made of palmetto tree trunks packed with deep sand, absorbed the force of iron cannonballs like a sponge. Rebel gun crews returned their own deliberate fire at the frigates. Gray gun smoke draped the fort. Moultrie puffed his pipe, pointing out targets and demanding that every shot hit home.

General Clinton soon recognized that the day, like the month and the season, was not going his way. As part of his promised diversion for Parker, he had launched the flat-bottomed flotilla seen by Moultrie that morning on Hamlin Creek. The boats drew close enough to Sullivan's Island to pepper Colonel Thomson's fortifications with sporadic gunfire, but rebel grapeshot and rifle fire forced Clinton to retreat. He tried several more attacks during the afternoon, to no avail.

Lee finally arrived at Fort Sullivan late in the afternoon to find the defenders "determined and cool to the last degree." Moultrie and his officers politely laid aside their pipes, answered his questions, requested more powder, and returned to the battle.

By early evening all hope for a British victory had vanished. Parker's frigates would fire some 7,000 rounds and burn more than 12 tons of powder compared to 960 rounds shot and 4,766 pounds burned for the Americans. Yet overwhelmingly the most damage had been dealt to the king's ships. As night fell, Parker signaled for the squadron to withdraw to their earlier moorings in Five-Fathom Hole. British battle casualties exceeded two hundred, including men wrecked beyond repair. Damage to British morale was also devastating. "The miscarriage," one of Clinton's officers conceded, "has greatly disheartened our troops." For the Americans, losses from the ten-hour bombardment totaled twenty-six wounded and twelve killed.

The victory at Sullivan's Island was a welcome tonic throughout the colonies after the discouraging news from Canada. It proved the Royal Navy vulnerable, thwarted British ambitions in the South, and boldly punctuated the new assertions of independence emanating from Philadelphia. "Glorious news from So. Carolina," a headline in the *Virginia Gazette* proclaimed. "Huzza!"

Now in retreat, Clinton urged Parker to forget South Carolina and to "lose no time in conveying the troops under my command to . . . William Howe" in the north.

EIGHTEEN

NEW YORK, NEW YORK

July–August 1776

The momentous news traveled swiftly on the post road from Philadelphia to New York, covering more than ninety miles and crossing five rivers in just a couple of days. Precise copies were made of the 1,300-word broadside titled "A Declaration" that arrived at the Mortier mansion headquarters, and by Tuesday, July 9, General Washington was ready for every soldier in his command to hear what Congress had to say. In his orders that morning, after affirming thirty-nine lashes for two convicted deserters, he instructed the army to assemble at 6:00 p.m. on various parade grounds, from Governors Island to King's Bridge. Each brigade major would then read—"with an audible voice"—the proclamation intended to transform a squalid family brawl into a cause as ambitious and righteous as any in human history.

> *We hold these truths to be self-evident, that all men are created equal, that they are endowed by their Creator with certain unalienable rights, that among these are life, liberty, and the pursuit of happiness.*

That to secure these rights, governments are instituted among men, deriving their just powers from the consent of the governed.

SEVERAL CONGRESSMEN, INCLUDING JOHN ADAMS, THOMAS JEFFERSON, AND BENJAMIN FRANKLIN, PRESENT THE DECLARATION OF INDEPENDENCE TO JOHN HANCOCK, THE PRESIDENT OF CONGRESS, IN PHILADELPHIA. *[LOC]*

Exuberant demonstrations erupted throughout the thirteen new states as word of the Declaration spread. Salutes and toasts followed publication of the document in the same issue of the *Virginia Gazette* that listed bounties for runaway enslaved people. In New Hampshire, mobs smashed tavern signs depicting a crown or the king's arms; some merchants refused coins with the king's likeness.

General Howe had an answer to the Declaration of Independence, and he sent it on Friday afternoon, July 12. Shortly after 3:00 p.m., British sailors on five warships weighed anchor off Staten Island, loosened and secured their sails, yanked the plugs from their gun muzzles, and sailed across the Upper Bay in brilliant sunshine. Led by the frigates *Phoenix* and *Rose*, with sixty-four guns between them, the squadron curled along the lower lip of Manhattan and opened fire at 4:05 p.m.

American gunners returned fire from the Star Redoubt and the Grenadier Battery, from Whitehall Battery and the Oyster Battery near Trinity Church. Flame stabbed through the screen of smoke blanketing the river and its banks. Only a few of the 196 American balls hit home; most fell short or flew wide.

By 4:30 p.m., the ships had run a gauntlet past eleven American batteries and had only scattered farmsteads north of the city to aim at. The enemy had breezed unhindered up the Hudson River, eluding defenses many months in the making, and was now anchored at Tappan Zee, thirty miles into the American rear.

As the Royal Navy outflanked rebel batteries on Manhattan Island, Howe moved into the Rose and Crown, a tavern built by Staten Island Huguenots more than a century earlier. He watched with satisfaction as the great bay stretching across to New York City gradually filled with the greatest war fleet Britain had ever launched, carrying the largest army the Crown had ever assembled. Until those reinforcements arrived, Howe was under orders from Lord Germain to delay his grand attack in order "that your force may be so increased as to render your success more certain." Yet each day that passed without the arrival of Clinton and Cornwallis from Charleston, and the German and British reinforcements from England, was another day lost in the campaign season.

On August 6, the New York Convention loaned Washington the fine telescope from King's College with the hope that it would be useful in "discovering the arrangements and operations of the enemy." Certainly there was much to see from a rooftop at the foot of Broadway: the 130 topsail vessels that had arrived from Halifax in

***BRITISH TROOPS ARRIVING IN NEW YORK** [NYPL]*

June with William Howe; the 150 additional sails that accompanied Admiral Richard Howe in July; the battered squadron of 45 vessels led by *Bristol* that arrived on August 1, reportedly carrying General Clinton from Charleston; and the 22-sail convoy that appeared on August 4 after a four-month voyage from the river Clyde in Scotland, carrying three thousand Highland soldiers.

On the late afternoon of August 12, yet another 107 ships slipped through the Narrows to be greeted with British cannon salutes. Aboard were a thousand guardsmen drawn from elite foot regiments often used to protect the king. Also aboard were more than 8,600 German troops—known collectively as Hessians, since most came from the landlocked, impoverished Hesse-Kassel region of Germany. They stood at the rails overjoyed to see land after fourteen weeks at sea.

Despite the spectacle that swam into view through the telescope eyepiece, Washington had no idea what the Howe brothers intended. His only meaningful intelligence came from deserters and escaped American prisoners, whose accounts often conflicted. In a newspaper distributed in New York, Washington cautioned that an enemy assault "may be hourly expected," and he urged "women, children, and infirm persons . . . to remove with all expedition." A depleted, skittish town grew emptier and more skittish.

Washington received an alarming note on August 15 from Nathanael Greene, newly promoted to major general and the commander of American defenses on Long Island. "I am confined to my bed with a raging fever," Greene wrote. Evacuated to a private home on Broadway in Manhattan, he would lie dangerously ill for two weeks while the commander in chief scrambled to find a replacement who knew something about how the army's left wing planned to fight.

✦✦✦

Aboard *Eagle*, the Howe brothers gathered with senior commanders for a final planning session. At first light on August 22, crimson columns of British soldiers marched from their tent camps to the Staten Island shoreline below the Watering Place. Many had already moved to staging locations on the warships and transports. In the Guards Brigade, each man carried a blanket, a bag with an extra shirt, and three days' provisions. Officers shouted out the articles of war to remind the men of dire consequences for those who failed to do their duty.

GENERAL WILLIAM HOWE LED BRITISH ARMY FORCES IN THE SUCCESSFUL CONQUEST OF NEW YORK. [LOC]

VICE ADMIRAL RICHARD HOWE, WILLIAM'S BROTHER, COMMANDED ROYAL NAVY FORCES IN AMERICA. [LOC]

Seventy-five flatboats had been assembled—each could carry more than five tons—plus eleven large bateaux and two galleys. Every boat had a number slathered on the bow and a flag denoting to which of ten landing divisions it belonged. At 8:00 a.m., a blue-and-white-striped flag appeared on the topmast of the command ship. A signal gun popped, and the invasion began. Before noon, 15,000 men had disembarked on Long Island, including 500 gunners with 40 field cannons, 1,500 Germans, and 120 light horse cavalrymen. Howe put his field headquarters a mile inland at Gravesend, and Hessians began leveling a road to move their artillery, peppering the adjacent woodlots with musket fire to discourage rebel snipers. Long Island loyalists emerged to greet the British and to serve as guides for the eventual drive on Brooklyn, a small village along the East River.

Washington struggled to sort through the breathless, contradictory reports from Long Island that were flooding his headquarters a few miles away on Manhattan Island. The commanding general promptly sent six regiments of reinforcements, but he waited a day, until Friday, August 23, before crossing the East River to judge for himself whether the British action was a full-on assault or a diversion. He could only guess.

He guessed wrong. He estimated that only eight thousand British troops were on Long Island, half the actual number. He thought that a larger force remained on Staten Island, staging for a possible strike at Manhattan. Washington dispatched four more Continental regiments, but he kept back much of his army to counter a phantom British blow.

Since his humiliating return from Charleston in early August, Henry Clinton had badgered General Howe with ideas for destroying Washington's army, preferably by outmaneuvering the Americans. Always eager to study the ground, he undertook something no Continental general had bothered to do: He carefully examined the terrain on western Long Island, including the remote bottomland stretching toward Jamaica. Having spent his boyhood in New York while his father was serving as the British governor, Clinton found the topography familiar, particularly with the help of fine British maps. His proposal, made two days before the attack from Staten Island, was as old as warfare: Fix the enemy in front with a robust diversion, then attack his flank. "That, once possessed, gives you the island," he promised.

At 9:00 p.m. on Monday, August 26, the British and their loyalist guides set off northeast from Flatlands, an old Dutch hamlet just inland from Jamaica Bay. Clinton left his campfires burning and his tents standing to deceive the rebels. Scattering flankers and skirmishers for security, he posted a regiment north of the road "for the purpose of drowning the noise of our cannon over the stones, masking our march, and preventing the enemy's patrols from discovering it." Even with the ranks closed up, the column stretched for nearly two miles under a rising moon. Cornwallis trailed Clinton, and was followed in turn by Howe and General Percy.

At 2:00 a.m. on Tuesday, a quarter mile from the Rising Sun tavern, Clinton sent forward a mounted patrol that soon returned

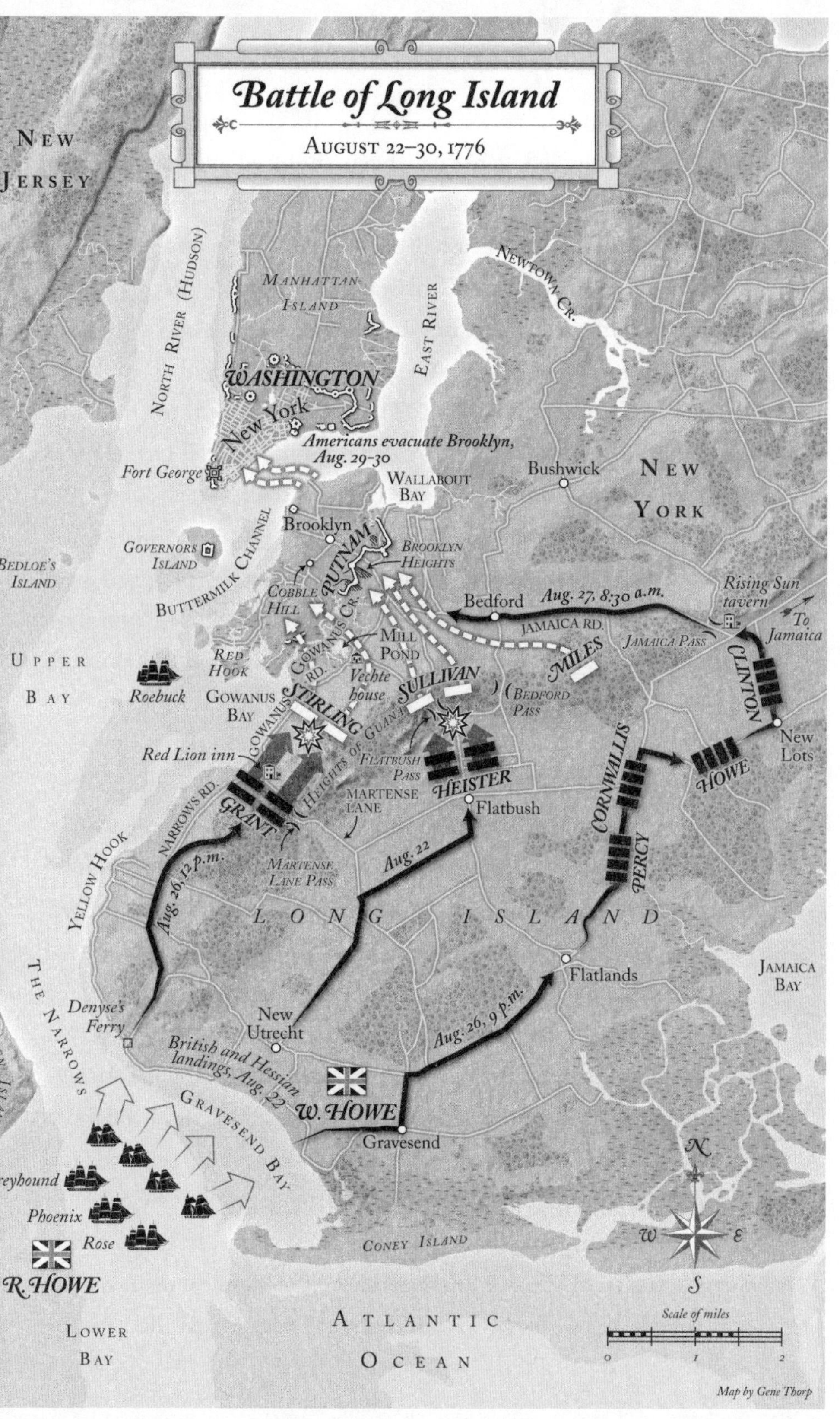

Battle of Long Island
August 22–30, 1776
New Jersey
North River (Hudson)
Manhattan Island
East River
Newtown Cr.
Washington
New York
Americans evacuate Brooklyn, Aug. 29-30
Fort George
Wallabout Bay
Bushwick
New York
Brooklyn
Governors Island
Bedloe's Island
Buttermilk Channel
Putnam
Brooklyn Heights
Cobble Hill
Gowanus Cr.
Bedford
Aug. 27, 8:30 a.m.
Rising Sun tavern
To Jamaica
Jamaica Rd.
Jamaica Pass
Mill Pond
Upper Bay
Red Hook
Roebuck
Gowanus Bay
Gowanus Rd.
Vechte house
Stirling
Sullivan
Miles
Bedford Pass
Clinton
New Lots
Red Lion inn
Gowanus
Heights of Guana
Flatbush Pass
Heister
Howe
Cornwallis
Narrows Rd.
Grant
Martense Lane
Flatbush
Yellow Hook
Aug. 26, 12 p.m.
Martense Lane Pass
Aug. 22
Percy
Long Island
The Narrows
Flatlands
Jamaica Bay
Denyse's Ferry
New Utrecht
Aug. 26, 9 p.m.
British and Hessian landings, Aug. 22
W. Howe
Gravesend
Gravesend Bay
Greyhound
Phoenix
Rose
R. Howe
Coney Island
N
W
E
S
Scale of miles
0
1
2
Lower Bay
Atlantic Ocean
Map by Gene Thorp

with five despondent prisoners. Rebel officers supposedly guarding the American left flank had been captured without firing a shot after mistaking the British horsemen for Americans. Clinton interrogated them, then rousted the tavern owner and his young son, whom he forced to guide his vanguard up a twisting, wooded bridle path across the ridge. Engineers widened the trail with saws rather than noisy axes, and extra horses were hitched to pull gun carriages to the brow of the hill. The column took three hours to move less than two miles. But by dawn Clinton's lead brigade had crossed the heights to straddle the Bedford road. Howe soon rode forward to join the front ranks.

Stray shooting belatedly alerted the Americans to trouble on their left. Colonel Samuel Miles, who commanded the Pennsylvania militia rifle regiment above Flatbush, hurried two miles through the woods to the Bedford road. "To my great mortification," he later wrote, "I saw the main body of the enemy in full march between me and our lines." A British force had covered ten miles in the dark to fall on the American rear by "a route we never dreamed of," a rifleman conceded. Fighting a losing action from hill to hill and tree to tree, Miles and more than 150 of his men would be captured. Others were shot dead or drowned trying to flee through ponds.

At 8:30 a.m., Clinton, Howe, and Cornwallis approached Bedford village, only two miles from the main rebel defenses in Brooklyn. Thirty minutes later two guns were fired in quick succession, signaling British forces on the Gowanus road and at Flatbush that the rebels were almost surrounded. The shots echoed and reechoed, like the sound of doom. The catastrophe had begun.

General Sullivan had also heard the signal guns, and the crackle of musketry from the rear. Across the heights, hundreds of Americans found British dragoons and light infantry across their escape paths. Caught between Clinton's column on the Bedford road and the Hessian and Highlander legions cascading over the heights, the Americans ran, hid, then ran some more, chased by whining bullets and shouting foes.

With the collapse of the American left and center, only General William Stirling's right wing remained intact. In the absence of orders from Sullivan or a defensive plan from Putnam, General Stirling began a fighting retreat only to realize that enemy grenadiers and Highlanders blocked the route to Brooklyn Heights. Hessians soon appeared on the slopes to his left, manning field guns to scorch the rebels. Stirling's command began to disintegrate. Soldiers bolted down game trails or hid from the Germans in hopes of surrendering to the British, believed to be less cruel.

Reduced to fewer than a thousand men, his command facing annihilation, Stirling quickly detached four hundred Marylanders to fight as a rear guard. The rest were to break through the British line as best they could. Stirling kept his men moving on the Gowanus road. Redcoats fell back to the Vechte farmhouse, a two-story fieldstone building with brick chimneys poking above the gables. Here the fiercest fighting of the day surged back and forth, as the Americans charged, fell back, and charged again in a swirl of smoke and singeing lead.

And then it ended. Cornwallis summoned reinforcements, Hessians and grenadiers pressed the rebel flanks with constant fire, and the din faded to a few random gunshots.

Washington had watched the final struggle from the crown of Cobble Hill, an elevation where a four-gun battery had been placed a mile northwest of the Vechte house. "Great God!" he was quoted as muttering. "What must my brave boys suffer today?"

On this hard day they had indeed suffered: General Howe would list almost 1,200 American prisoners taken, including three generals, three colonels, and four lieutenant colonels, plus thirty-two cannons seized. Howe estimated the total American casualties, including killed and wounded, at 3,300. No battle in the eight-year war would be larger in the number of combatants—more than 40,000, naval forces included—and few would be more lopsided.

For the Americans, defeat brought discouragement and exhaustion. Soldiers doubted their field officers; field officers doubted their generals. Finger-pointing abounded. Faith in General Washington fell. Such doubts were justified. The commanding general had misread the battlefield and botched the battle. Though Congress wanted New York defended, Washington had failed to recognize that holding Long Island—the key to holding New York—would be impossible with a weak, divided, overmatched army that lacked naval power. For the moment, his country and his soldiers tried to regroup and remain determined.

At 5:00 p.m. on Thursday, August 29, Washington summoned eight of his generals to Four Chimneys, a large house in Brooklyn a few steps from the river. The commanding general wasted no time in putting the question: whether "under all circumstances it would not be [better] to leave Long Island and its dependencies, and remove the army to New York?" Without dissent, his lieutenants voted to evacuate.

One by one Washington's regiments withdrew from the line on Thursday night and shuffled toward the ferry landing above Four Chimneys. By early Friday, watermen were evacuating a thousand soldiers an hour, each vessel so laden that the sides sat just inches above the black water. Back and forth the boats shuttled, silent but for the odd creak of a tiller or an ungreased oarlock. At 2:00 a.m., a fogbank settled over Brooklyn, masking the effort. The last boats

GEORGE WASHINGTON'S FORCES WERE OUTFLANKED ON LONG ISLAND AND FORCED TO RETREAT IN DISARRAY. *[LOC]*

glided through the gray mist toward Manhattan. One of them carried General Washington.

Back in the Mortier house, Washington slept the sleep of the saved, confident that he had rescued his army and redeemed his reputation. "Never was a greater feat of generalship shown than in this retreat," Lieutenant Colonel James Chambers, a Pennsylvanian, told his wife, "to bring off an army of twelve thousand men, within sight of a strong enemy possessed of as strong a fleet as ever floated on our seas, without any loss, and saving all the baggage."

THE CONTINENTAL ARMY'S RETREAT FROM LONG ISLAND. *[LOC]*

Long Island was lost—for seven years and two months, as it turned out—and the American hold on Manhattan seemed tenuous. A day later, Washington's chief engineer, Colonel Rufus Putnam, warned him, "I have reconnoitered every part about the island of New York and . . . find the enemy have such a variety of places to choose out of, that it's impossible to prevent their landing when they please."

NINETEEN

NEW YORK, NEW YORK

September 1776

Partly as a concession to the British citizens who still hoped for a negotiated settlement, King George in the spring had reluctantly agreed to appoint brothers General William Howe and Admiral Richard Howe as peace commissioners in a last-ditch attempt to end the war. For months the cabinet had argued over how far the Howes could go in making a deal; in the end, it was not far at all. Twenty-four paragraphs of instructions issued in May directed that no overall pardons be given or concessions offered until the rebels dissolved Congress and their state assemblies, disbanded their armies, surrendered all forts, guaranteed compensation to injured loyalists, and agreed not to tax British imports.

At 2:00 p.m. on Wednesday, September 11, Richard Howe stood on a sandy beach just below the Billopp mansion, a fieldstone manor house built on the southwestern nob of Staten Island. His brother William was busy preparing the army's return to action, so the admiral would handle today's encounter alone.

A quarter mile across Arthur Kill, Howe's barge—trimmed in red and gold—pulled away from Perth Amboy, on the New Jersey shore. A white flag snapped from the bow. Between the straining navy bargemen sat three skeptical men sent by Congress to hear the admiral's pitch. Even at a distance Howe recognized the broad shoulders and domed forehead of the senior American in the trio. He and Dr. Benjamin Franklin had met half a dozen times in London.

Franklin stepped from the barge, bowed, and introduced his two companions. The plump, short man with a tangle of graying hair was John Adams, now forty, a member of more than two dozen congressional committees and president of the new Continental Board of War and Ordnance. The other was Edward Rutledge, just twenty-six, a London-trained lawyer from South Carolina.

ADMIRAL RICHARD HOWE MEETS THREE DELEGATES FROM CONGRESS—BENJAMIN FRANKLIN, JOHN ADAMS, AND EDWARD RUTLEDGE—AT STATEN ISLAND, NEW YORK, IN AN UNSUCCESSFUL PEACE CONFERENCE. [WIKIMEDIA COMMONS]

The men chatted civilly for half an hour around a large table, nibbling on cold ham, tongue, and mutton washed down with red wine. Then Howe ordered the table cleared and opened the discussion.

The "declaration of independency" complicated his task, he said, because he had no authority "to consider the colonies in the light of independent states." Nor could he acknowledge Congress as a legitimate body. Therefore, he must negotiate with his guests not as congressmen but "merely as gentlemen of ability and influence" whom he hoped would help "put a stop to the calamities of war."

The king's "most earnest desire [is] to make his American subjects happy," he continued, but that required giving up the idea of independence. If the Americans "return to their allegiance and obedience to the government of Great Britain," it was possible they could control their own legislation and taxes. America might again provide "solid advantages" to the empire in commerce and manpower.

The discussion meandered, faltered, and grew repetitive. When Howe urged "a stop to these ruinous extremities," Franklin shot back: "Forces have been sent out and towns have been burnt. We cannot now expect happiness under the domination of Great Britain. All former attachments have been obliterated."

Finding no agreement possible after three hours of talk, Howe walked his guests back to his barge and watched as they glided through late-afternoon shadows toward the far shore.

Franklin, ever the finger-drumming chess player, was thinking of his next move, and the moves after that. A close look at the British anchorage in New York persuaded him that a French armada from Brest and Toulon could destroy even the formidable Admiral Howe. That would require France to wholeheartedly join the American cause as a military ally.

Howe felt deflated as he returned to his flagship, the *Eagle*. "The three gentlemen were very explicit in their opinions that the associated colonies would not accede to any peace or alliance but as free and independent states," he wrote Lord Germain from his cabin. "The conversation ended, and the gentlemen returned to Amboy."

His secretary was more succinct. "They met, they talked, they parted," Ambrose Serle told his journal. "And now nothing remains but to fight it out."

In early September, General Greene had urged Washington to abandon Manhattan, noting that they had long agreed that the city "would not be tenable if the enemy got possession of Long Island and Governors Island." A few days later, when Washington put the issue to a war council at his Mortier headquarters, a majority resisted evacuation, not least because Congress had just affirmed its hope to retain New York undamaged. Instead they agreed on a weak tactical compromise that would scatter the army in three divisions across sixteen miles: five thousand to hold the city under General Putnam, nine thousand under General William Heath to defend King's Bridge, at the northern tip of Manhattan, and, in between, various militia regiments along the East River.

Now the British had both Governor's Island and Long Island. On Thursday, September 12, a day after the peace conference on Staten Island, the commander in chief summoned his generals to McGowan's tavern, just south of Harlem on the road from King's Bridge. This time they voted ten to three to evacuate New York

NEW YORK CITY HARBOR. [NYPL]

City, retracting the army to Harlem Heights—a rocky plateau protected by a steep slope facing south—and packing eight thousand men onto the high ground at Fort Washington along the Hudson.

After further consideration of the difficulty of defending New York, Congress had belatedly agreed to abandon the city, but refused to authorize arson. Instead Washington ordered the town stripped. Bells were lowered from church belfries and public buildings, then ferried to Newark to be melted down by cannon foundries. Horse teams hauled provisions to King's Bridge; war stocks that could not be moved were dumped in the river or burned on the shoreline. Sloops and wagons evacuated the sick to New Jersey or Westchester County, to the north.

Before dawn on Sunday, September 15, the ominous rattle of anchor chains could be heard by five hundred Connecticut troops dug in along Kip's Bay, a shallow indentation on the Manhattan shoreline, five miles up the East River from the Grand Battery. Many of the militiamen had been in the army for just a few weeks. Some carried only pikes or pickaxes, which would be of little use this morning.

Daylight revealed five men-of-war moored bow to stern, their gun ports open, just three hundred yards from the beach. A hushed calm persisted until 10:00 a.m., when eighty-four flatboats carrying four thousand British and German troops spilled from Newtown Creek, a twisting inlet across the river.

Just past the stroke of eleven, the cannonade began, broadside after broadside ripping from seventy guns. By noon, when the signal was given for the bombardment to stop and the flatboats to advance in four columns, many rebels had already scurried up the slope to the rear. British light infantry companies surged to the right through the now empty Connecticut camp, and grenadiers led by Cornwallis made for rising ground in the center beyond the beach.

Washington had raced seven miles from his new headquarters toward the sound of the guns. He now sat on his horse in a farm lane a thousand yards northwest of Kip's Bay, conferring with Generals Putnam and Parsons about how to keep the British from pushing north. Hundreds of panting men, with muskets and without, rushed away from the East River. "Take the walls!" Washington shouted at them. "Take the corn field!" Some tried to form a hasty defensive line, but "in a most confused and disordered manner," Parsons acknowledged.

A few hundred yards to the south, a small cluster of redcoats appeared. Nothing Washington or the other generals did could convince their troops to stand and face the enemy. Washington, furious and distraught, eventually trotted west to the Bloomingdale Road. All around him groups of soldiers drifted across pastures and down cart paths, away from the enemy.

An American column of 3,500 men snaked from the city at midafternoon on Sunday for the twelve-mile march along the Hudson toward Harlem Heights. Three British warships—*Renown*, *Repulse*, and *Pearl*—had hurried the evacuation by lobbing a few broadsides into the town. Dressed in a sleeveless vest over a dirty shirt, General Putnam rode up and down the line astride a wild-eyed, foaming horse, barking encouragement and urging speed.

Left behind in New York were the entrenchments, redoubts, and ditches built over the past eight months but now useless. Also abandoned was over half of Washington's heavy artillery—sixty-four guns, including fifteen mounted thirty-two-pounders—and twelve thousand rounds of shot, enough to replenish the dwindling British naval ammunition stocks.

Washington had lost another battle, most of another island, and his first city. American casualties in what he called "this disgraceful and dastardly" retreat included about 50 killed and, according to a British tally, 371 captured.

Jubilant loyalists sporting red ribbons emerged from New York cellars welcoming their liberators with shouts of "God save the king!"

Monday, September 16, brought the rebels a modest measure of redemption and self-respect. Washington had planned three roughly parallel defensive lines north of the craggy Harlem Heights cliffs, with the new, five-sided Fort Washington even farther up the island. About ten thousand fit-to-fight men crowded these wooded uplands, and another six thousand occupied King's Bridge and crossings into Westchester County. General Greene's three brigades held the southernmost line, which featured a trio of small redoubts where Manhattan narrowed into its northern panhandle. Two miles away, enemy campfires flickered from meadows near the future Central Park.

Before first light, on Washington's orders, a patrol of 120 men slipped below the lines through the thick forest fronting the Hudson River. They were Rangers, a New England troop led by Lieutenant Colonel Thomas Knowlton, newly created for scouting and moving silently in woods. At daybreak, British sentries on Bloomingdale Road spied shadows darting through the trees. Shots flew back and forth. Four hundred regulars scampered up the road to confront the intruders until the Rangers rose from behind a stone wall and threw a scorching volley at fifty yards' range. For half an hour the

***LIEUTENANT COLONEL THOMAS KNOWLTON, THE LEADER OF THE RANGERS.** [NYPL]*

foes traded gunshots. Thousands of bullets nipped leaves and punctured tree trunks before Knowlton retreated, pressed hard by redcoats. Each side had suffered about ten casualties.

Alerted to the gunfire, Washington rode to the rim of the heights. He had concocted a small, vengeful plan. Serving as decoys, some 150 volunteers from Greene's division scrambled down the bluff to a salt marsh, then fell back a few hundred yards as the eager British rushed forward, firing on the run. Washington fed the rest of the brigade into the brawl—eventually totaling nine hundred men—to keep the enemy focused. Meanwhile, Knowlton and his Rangers, joined by three Virginia rifle companies under Major Andrew Leitch, circled across a rock outcropping to the east, intent on ambushing the British detachment from behind.

The ambush only harassed the redcoats, and both Knowlton and Leitch were mortally wounded by gunfire. But by noon the British had fallen back a mile to a buckwheat field, dragging their dead and wounded, pressed by nearly two thousand rebels. The American line stood four deep in places—firing and loading, firing and loading. The crackle of musketry merged into an unbroken roar. Smoke, reddened by muzzle flashes, rolled across the landscape with each new volley. Officers cautioned their men not to shoot until they could see the enemy's feet through the smoke.

The British fell back again at 3:00 p.m., their ammunition dwindling, but with Howe's reserves now piling into the fight. Wary

THE BATTLE OF HARLEM HEIGHTS. *[NYPL]*

of being outflanked to the east, Washington halted the pursuit and ordered his men to make their way back up the heights. A few final shots rang out, and the battlefield fell silent.

The small victory in a minor skirmish proved a boost for the Americans. "Every visage was seen to lighten," one colonel commented. The troops had slugged it out at forty yards' range against British regulars, Highlanders, and Hessians, advancing and withdrawing with reasonable discipline. "This affair I am in hopes will be attended with many salutary consequences," Washington wrote to John Hancock, "as it seems to have greatly inspirited the whole of our troops."

TWENTY

NEW YORK, NEW YORK

September 21, 1776

No persuasive evidence ever emerged that the fires incinerating much of New York had been set deliberately. Shortly after midnight on Saturday, September 21, a blaze began in a bar called the Fighting Cocks at Whitehall Slip, near the Grand Battery. Some claimed the tavern was occupied by careless drunks; others said that British soldiers' wives were burning pine boards when a chimney fire ignited. A captured Pennsylvania soldier held aboard *Pearl* in the harbor described seeing flames dancing along the waterfront. Driven by a brisk southerly breeze, the fire spread to the north and west, yet no bells clanged in alarm since they all had been hauled off to rebel cannon works. Hundreds of terrified New Yorkers

NEW YORK CITY BURNING IN SEPTEMBER 1776. [LOC]

sought sanctuary on the open land of the Common, cowering as flames licked through the town.

An abrupt change in wind direction and a natural firebreak formed by the open terrain at King's College just north of Trinity Church caused the flames to subside on Saturday morning. Within a mile-long charred swath, some five hundred houses had been reduced to ash, about a quarter of the city's total. Most docks, warehouses, and commercial buildings were spared, Governor Tryon told Lord Germain, although many small shopkeepers were burned out.

TRINITY CHURCH, WHICH WAS DESTROYED IN THE FIRE OF 1776. *[NYPL]*

The British suspected arson. British authorities reportedly detained two hundred suspects, but all were released despite rewards offered for incriminating testimony. Seven years later, a British commission failed to resolve whether the fire was accidental, deliberate, or a combination of both, although it was generally agreed that no American order led to the city's burning. In September 1776, however, those about to spend the winter in a badly charred town believed the worst of the American high command.

Washington, for his part, considered the fire a fortunate occurrence. "Had I been left to the dictates of my own judgment, New York should have been laid in ashes before I quitted it. To this end I applied to Congress, but was absolutely forbid," he told his overseer at Mount Vernon. "Providence, or some good honest fellow, has done more for us than we were disposed to do for ourselves."

TWENTY-ONE

BRITISH ARTILLERY PARK, FIVE MILES NORTH OF NEW YORK

September 22, 1776

On September 22, a young American officer captured out of uniform on Long Island waited for the hangman to summon him to his death. Captain Nathan Hale, twenty-one years old, had enlisted in the army in 1775, served at the siege of Boston, and marched to New York with his regiment. Hale had recently joined Knowlton's Rangers as a company commander, and when the high command sought a volunteer to spy incognito behind the British lines on Long Island, Hale stepped forward. Dressed in a brown summer suit and pretending to be a traveling loyalist schoolteacher, Hale carried his Yale diploma as a credential.

Precisely what Hale did during his brief career as a secret agent after crossing Long Island Sound in mid-September, and how he was found out, would remain unknown. Some would claim that he was exposed by a loyalist who recognized him or that he was detained while attempting to slip back across the East River during the great fire. Regardless, incriminating notes and sketches were found hidden in Hale's shoes.

Howe ordered Hale to be executed in the morning. Much would be made of Hale's last words, and admirers later credited him with a line paraphrased from Joseph Addison's play *Cato*, loved by those yearning for liberty: "I only regret that I have but one life to lose for my country."

Hale's corpse was left dangling for several days as a gruesome warning, and above him British soldiers suspended a board upon which they painted the figure of a soldier and scribbled *George Washington*.

THE EXECUTION OF CAPTAIN NATHAN HALE IN NEW YORK. *[LOC]*

TWENTY-TWO

NEW YORK, NEW YORK

October–November 1776

From the wide porch of the Roger Morris house on Harlem Heights, General Washington could see all too clearly both the ground he had already lost to the British and the terrain now at risk. Built more than a decade earlier on Manhattan's second-highest hill by a loyalist who had since fled to London, the nineteen-room mansion offered a panoramic vista of New York, Brooklyn, and Staten Island far to the south, as well as the Hudson River and New Jersey to the west and, to the north and east, Westchester County and the Long Island Sound. American soldiers controlled roughly half of the landscape visible to their commanding general from his high perch, but few doubted that the brothers Howe coveted a larger share before winter set in.

THE ROGER MORRIS HOUSE ON HARLEM HEIGHTS SERVED AS GENERAL WASHINGTON'S HEADQUARTERS FOR SEVERAL WEEKS. [LOC]

The grumble of heavy artillery along the Hudson River early on Wednesday morning, October 9, ended the unspoken truce of the past three weeks. After an initial raid upriver, the Royal Navy for weeks had been content to position several men-of-war along General Howe's left flank below Harlem Heights, seven miles upstream from the Grand Battery. Now a trio of vessels—*Phoenix*, *Roebuck*, and *Tartar*—weighed anchor at seven o'clock on the early tide and swept north, intent on again reclaiming the Hudson River for the King.

Within twenty minutes, five American batteries above the Manhattan shoreline and two more in New Jersey had found the range. Cannon fire ripped across the Hudson and great splashes leaped up around the ships.

Washington's engineers had continued their ingenious if unrealistic efforts to blockade the river, both with fortifications ashore and with obstructions underwater. The Hudson was, in fact, vaster than the Americans realized. Two surveyors using a seven-pound lead weight had reported that the waters off Fort Washington were no deeper than seven fathoms, or forty-two feet. They miscalculated: A wide channel along Jeffrey's Hook, where the George Washington Bridge would later stand, was twelve fathoms, an abyss capable of swallowing whatever was dumped into it. In late September, Washington had learned that the obstructions "sunk in the river may not be sufficient for stopping the enemy's ships." New soundings were ordered "with all the secrecy possible."

Too late. At 9:00 a.m. that Wednesday, Captain Hyde Parker swung *Roebuck* into the channel brushing the Manhattan shoreline. As the cannonade sounded, Parker nosed the flotilla to within forty yards of the nearest battery where the channel ran deepest. Within an hour the squadron had slipped through the gauntlet to fire at rebel rivercraft upstream.

At 5:00 p.m., after scorching the riverfront with broadsides, Captain Parker and his squadron anchored in Tappan Zee. Farmers and fishermen fled inland; militiamen peeped through the trees for signs of redcoat regiments disembarking. The British had sailed through the river obstructions "as if they were cobwebs," by one account. "To our surprise and mortification," lamented Colonel Tench Tilghman, a Washington aide, "they all ran through without the least difficulty and without receiving any apparent damage from our forts."

Once again a hostile British force was in Washington's rear, controlling the Hudson River for thirty miles even as General Howe's force inched up the East River toward Long Island Sound. Upper Manhattan, King's Bridge, and Westchester seemed at risk.

But completely surrounding the Americans would require a military genius beyond William Howe's capacity. Able, sensible, and often plodding, the British commander seemed unsure of his course even though he now had the upper hand in New York. Washington's position in Manhattan seemed too strong to attack frontally, and, the British commander complained, "innumerable difficulties are in our way of turning him on either side"—much less both sides. Howe's earlier conviction that destroying the rebel army in decisive battle would be "the most effectual means to terminate this expensive war" had evolved into a more cautious approach of outmaneuvering Washington, occupying rebel territory, then maneuvering again.

To that end, at 3:00 p.m. on Friday, October 11, Howe's

regiments began to strike their tents and prepare for a modest flanking move to Frog's Neck, a narrow peninsula jutting southeast into the mouth of Long Island Sound. Staff officers gathered at 5:00 p.m. in the Dove Tavern for final orders, and at 10:00 p.m., the sleepy troops marched to their boats with the usual clattering kit and muttered curses. At daybreak on Saturday, the first wave of the assault force pushed off on the morning tide with artillery vessels, horse and troop transports, and men-of-war.

By midday, four thousand nauseous soldiers had regained dry land at Frog's Neck, with twice that number bobbing close behind. Reassembled by regiment, the redcoat column soon stepped off a track that led to the road toward King's Bridge, six miles northwest.

Only now did the folly of General Howe's scheme come clear. At high tide, the two-mile-long peninsula became an island, and rebel troops had torn planks from the connecting bridge. Past the bridge, near a mill on the far side of the inlet, twenty-five riflemen under Major William S. Smith crouched behind a tall stack of firewood. A blistering first volley sent Howe's advance troops diving for cover. Shots flew back and forth; the regulars built hasty breastworks and searched in vain for an unguarded shallow crossing. Stone walls between pastures prevented British gunners from hauling up their artillery and ammunition wagons except on the bullet-swept road.

By nightfall 11,000 British soldiers with sixteen field guns were bottled up on the peninsula by 1,800 Americans with fewer guns but better ground.

Washington had been oblivious to the danger on his left flank. He made no move to evacuate the now vulnerable lines at Harlem Heights or to counter Howe's gambit by fortifying more high ground in Westchester. A more discerning battle captain would soon arrive to show the commanding general the error of his ways.

Like a conquering hero, Major General Charles Lee crossed the Hudson into Westchester County on Monday, October 14, at the end of his march north from Charleston. The ranks were thrilled to see him, and word of his arrival aroused "the universal satisfaction of the camp," a New Jersey chaplain wrote. "We expect soon a stroke that will decide the victory of this campaign." Lee promptly recognized that any such stroke likely would come from the enemy: Frog's Neck could not long hold out against the British. He implored Washington to immediately withdraw most of his force from Manhattan into Westchester to avoid being surrounded. The commander in chief listened attentively, as appreciative as usual of Lee's tactical advice. On Wednesday, he and fifteen of his generals gathered at Lee's new headquarters to furiously debate the matter before voting almost unanimously to retreat north.

Thirteen thousand American soldiers trudged north out of Manhattan and from around King's Bridge in a slow, winding column along the west bank of the Bronx River. A rear guard set fire to abandoned barracks and camp stores. So many wagons and teams had been lost in the past two months that the men pulled much of their baggage and even artillery by hand, or shuttled them in tedious relays along farm roads. Herdsmen and militia companies drove hogs, sheep, and cattle onto the Westchester flatlands. Few provisions were to be found in the county except for buckwheat, potatoes, and some corn—soldiers and camp followers continued to plunder without pause—and quartermasters asked New York authorities for thirty thousand bushels of grain, a thousand tons of hay, and as many horses and oxen as possible.

At 1:00 a.m. on Friday, October 18, Howe moved again, although not far and not gracefully. Four thousand grenadiers, light infantry, and German Jäger (infantrymen) embarked in two hundred flatboats from the western shore of Frog's Neck, then sailed by moonlight three miles north to Pell's Point. Landing unopposed and apparently undetected, the assault force with six field guns by midmorning had trudged more than a mile inland on a country lane, relieved to find neither enemy riflemen nor a vandalized bridge blocking their progress.

Yet watching through a spyglass from a nearby hilltop was a man who would spoil Howe's day. Colonel John Glover of Marblehead, Massachusetts, had command of the 14th Continental Regiment. He and his men had been largely responsible for the stealthy evacuation of Washington's army from Brooklyn two months earlier. With not a moment to lose, he sent forward a captain and forty men to pester the British front ranks. A loud, smoky volley from American muskets, fowling pieces, and squirrel rifles was followed by four more volleys before Glover ordered the company to retreat. Enemy infantrymen rushed forward, but at thirty yards' range, two hundred Massachusetts troops from the 13th Continental popped up from behind a stone wall on the left side of the lane. As one they fired, and a whizzing swarm of lead shredded the British advance. "The enemy broke," Glover reported.

Howe's troops collected themselves before surging forward again, this time also pounding the American line

COLONEL JOHN GLOVER.
[WIKIMEDIA COMMONS]

with cannon fire. More volleys swept back and forth, seventeen in all from the 3rd Continental before they, too, leapfrogged to the rear. At noon, Glover spotted British troops under General Cornwallis moving along the shoreline around the American left flank. The colonel signaled retreat. Howe chose not to pursue, and thus forfeited another chance to smash his enemy.

Howe had White Plains, the site of the rebels' main storehouses, in his sights. An advance guard of two thousand men crept forward, halting each night on secure ground fortified with artillery. Behind them, hired teamsters cracked their whips and Royal Navy gunners came ashore to help shoulder the fieldpieces from one ridge to the next. Still the army would need ten days to move seventeen miles.

Step by slow step, Howe's avenging force of nineteen thousand came on. Farmers handed cider and milk to passing redcoats, hoping to curry favor. The British commander placed his headquarters in a tavern on the Boston post road in Eastchester, and on Friday, October 25, two columns began their final approaches toward White Plains: General Leopold Philip de Heister on the left, along the Bronx River past Scarsdale, and General Clinton on the right. By Sunday, the army had converged on a front stretching several miles from east to west, with enemy high ground ahead. That night the Hessians built enormous campfires from flax stubble to make their strength seem even more formidable. Officers ordered artillery horses driven back and forth, dragging chains to suggest the arrival of siege guns.

For more than a week, allowed by Howe's slow advance, the Americans had gathered at White Plains. Just over thirteen thousand fit-for-duty men now held this stony high ground. Early on Monday, October 28, Washington rode west with Lee for a closer look at his right wing. As they surveyed the terrain, a horseman raced up to announce, "The British are on the camp, sir." The commanding general galloped back to his headquarters, where his advisor Colonel Joseph Reed confirmed that Howe's brigades were barely a mile to the south, having swatted aside the American sentries. "Gentlemen," Washington told his officers, "you will repair to your respective posts, and do the best you can."

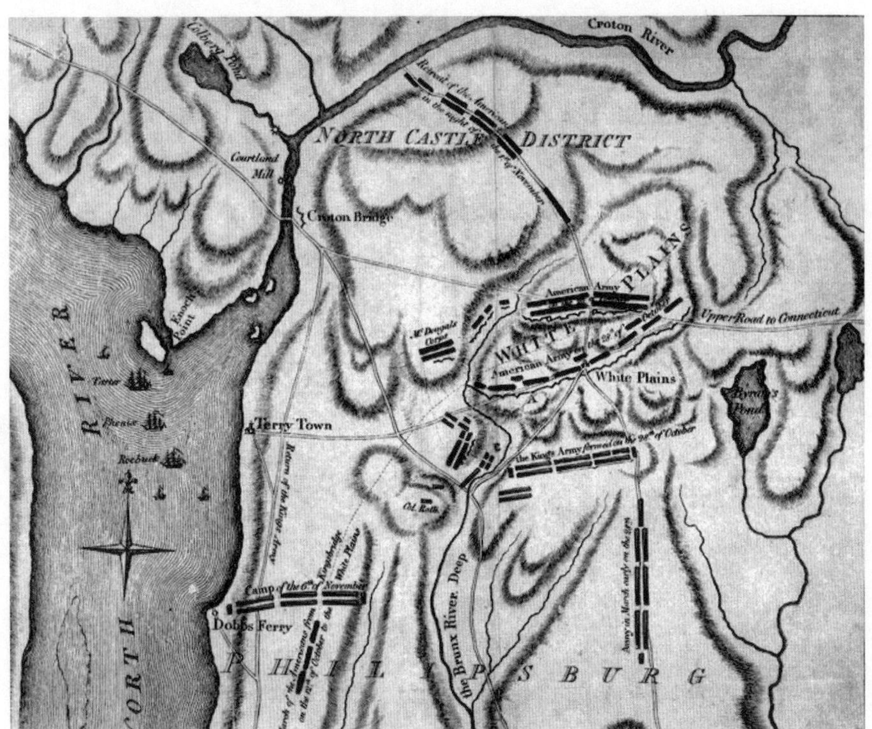

THE BATTLE PLAN AT WHITE PLAINS. BOTH ARMIES' MOVEMENTS ARE SHOWN. *[NYPL]*

From Purdy Hill, the spectacle was bewitching: Thirteen thousand enemy troops emerged from the wood line in impeccable oblong formations of red and blue, bayonets gleaming, horses prancing, a hundred banners and pennants barely stirring in the still morning. Two columns divided into eight, and the noise of regimental bands carried across the plain, punctuated by pounding drums and full-throated Hessian grenadiers singing some war ballad.

To disrupt this fine parade, Washington ordered Major General Joseph Spencer to push forward with two thousand troops as a blocking force along the muddy Bronx River. Their muzzle flashes drew enemy artillery fire. A bold charge by Hessian grenadiers was stopped by a New England volley that "scattered them like leaves in a whirlwind," one officer wrote. Then light dragoons appeared with their sabers drawn, and the rebel retreat turned into a rout. Flailing men splashed across the river and into the woods beyond.

Only this morning, during his aborted reconnaissance ride, Washington, prodded by Lee, had recognized the vulnerability of his right flank. Chatterton Hill, a steep hardwood ridge, rose almost two hundred feet above the Bronx River, half a mile west of the Continental line. If the British overpowered militia outposts atop this commanding height, their guns could rake American defenses at White Plains and beyond. Washington ordered the hill reinforced with the Delaware regiment commanded by John Haslet. No sooner had the colonel and his men gained the Chatterton summit than a Hessian cannonade pounded the hill. The militia, sheltering behind stone walls and breastworks built of cornstalk clumps, fled. More American reinforcements arrived at midday in a brigade of Connecticut, New York, Massachusetts, and Maryland regiments under Brigadier General Alexander McDougall, who now commanded two thousand men on Chatterton's Hill.

General Howe sat on his horse in a field of wheat stubble along the river, eyeing the hill looming half a mile to the north. Couriers on sweating mounts galloped off with new orders, and just before 1:00 p.m., the British attack tilted to the American right. Hessian engineers cut down trees and collected fence rails to bridge the river. Two British foot regiments crossed at a ford downstream, then scrambled up the lower slopes, only to be slapped back by rebel fire. Howe pushed more reserves into the attack, including dragoons, grenadiers, and another German brigade, bringing the assault force to seven thousand.

By midafternoon, blue-coated Hessians had emerged from the smoke to form a skirmish line on Chatterton's southwest brow. Now the Continental regiments buckled—retreating, shooting, retreating. Rebel bodies covered the hilltop. After forming in regiments, the British and Hessians threw up hasty fortifications, then built great barnwood fires to dry their sodden uniforms before lying on their arms for the night.

Washington shortened his lines and braced for the next blow, but teeming rains on Wednesday night mired the roads and forced a British postponement. By the time new attack orders went out, the rebels had turned back a mile into the rugged upcountry at North Castle.

The Westchester campaign sputtered to a close. On the night of November 2, American sentries heard the unmistakable clank of departing enemy artillery carriages; within two days the British and Hessians had abandoned their holdings from Chatterton Hill through White Plains. Howe sensibly saw no profit in chasing rebels through broken country without any hope of enticing them into a decisive battle.

TWENTY-THREE

FORT WASHINGTON, NEW YORK, AND FORT LEE, NEW JERSEY

November 16–20, 1776

Looming 265 feet above the Hudson, with steep slopes on three sides, Fort Washington, the last rebel outpost on Manhattan Island, gave the illusion that it was unconquerable. Several outposts were meant to protect the approaches and forty-seven cannons had been moved into position, from three- to thirty-two-pounders; teams of twenty-two oxen pulled the heaviest guns up to the citadel. For months, dust-caked soldiers had wielded axes, shovels, and pickaxes to strengthen the five-sided fort's dirt ramparts. But the fortress could not be effectively defended: Rebel engineers lacked the gunpowder to blast deep trenches and other fortifications to keep attackers at bay. It also had no water and no reservoir; a well started in early summer had been abandoned, and every drop had to be hauled up in buckets from the Hudson River. The guns, if impressive in number, had failed to stop British ships from traversing the river—the only reason for the fort to exist in the first place.

A PLAQUE MARKING THE FALL OF FORT WASHINGTON, THE LAST AMERICAN TOEHOLD ON MANHATTAN ISLAND. *[LOC]*

The British high command knew with precision the weaknesses both of their opponents and of the fort. Letters from Washington to Congress had been intercepted in late October when a careless courier left his satchel unattended; they revealed poor discipline, inadequate officers, and other details. Moreover, seventeen deserters had abandoned Fort Washington in recent weeks with specific information about the thin American defenses, ammunition levels, and faltering morale.

Washington, by contrast, had little insight into British intentions. He speculated that Howe "must attempt something on account of his reputation, for what has he done as yet with his great army?" What to do with his own army puzzled him too. After consulting his war council, the commander in chief split the force into four parts: General Heath would post the Hudson Highlands upriver with four thousand men; Lee was to remain in Westchester with seven thousand to block approaches into upstate New York and New England; Major General Nathanael Greene's detachment in New Jersey would grow to several thousand, scattered at various strong points; and Colonel Robert Magaw was left clinging to Fort Washington by his fingernails.

At 11:00 a.m. on Sunday, November 10, Washington cantered

northwest from his camp above White Plains to begin a winding journey that would last the rest of the year. Late on Wednesday afternoon, Washington arrived at Greene's tidy headquarters in a house beneath a pine tree on the lane leading from Fort Lee to Burdett's Ferry. Greene would earn acclaim as one of the finest commanders in American military history. At thirty-four, he was the youngest Continental general and already a Washington favorite for his decisive mind, rigorous discipline, and devotion to both the cause and the commander in chief. For two days, Washington studied the Hudson, the fortifications, and the American positions, swayed by Greene and others despite his own misgivings. Round and round the debate swirled. "His Excellency General Washington has been with me for several days," Greene wrote to Knox. "The evacuation or reinforcement of Fort Washington was under consideration, but finally nothing concluded on." Washington later acknowledged a "warfare in my mind, and hesitation."

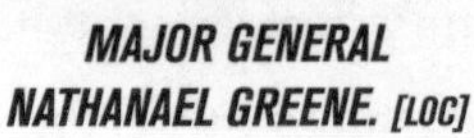

MAJOR GENERAL NATHANAEL GREENE. ***[LOC]***

No hesitation troubled William Howe's mind. The chance to seize several thousand rebels and destroy their last stronghold on Manhattan Island was too enticing. At 1:00 p.m. on Friday, November 15, a mounted British officer carrying a white flag trotted from King's Bridge up the steep, dusty ramp to Fort Washington. Lieutenant Colonel James Patterson, Howe's adjutant general, carried a simple ultimatum, which he handed to the American officer sent to intercept him: The rebel garrison was to surrender within two hours or every man would be put to the sword. Magaw, whose headquarters was in the Morris house on Harlem Heights, scribbled a defiant reply—"Actuated by the most glorious cause that mankind ever fought in, I am determined to defend the post to the very last extremity"—then sent a courier across the Hudson with copies of this correspondence for Greene and a request for advice.

Greene, in turn, wrote to Washington, who was now in Hackensack, for advice. The last hint of daylight had long faded by the time the commanding general crossed the Hackensack River and galloped by dim moonlight to the Hudson dock below Fort Lee, another rebel stronghold on the New Jersey shoreline. Stepping into a barge, he ordered the crew to stroke for the far shore, where the black silhouette of Fort Washington could be seen crowning the dark ridgeline a mile to the east. Halfway across the Hudson, a shadow emerged from other shadows, and a westbound skiff carrying Greene and General Israel Putnam pulled alongside. The officers conferred in urgent tones. Magaw seemed in good spirits, Greene reported, and was determined to hold out indefinitely. He and Putnam had approved Magaw's defensive scheme, then wished him luck. Nothing more could be done until dawn.

As the sun rose the next morning, Washington was in a boat with Greene and Putnam. The first booming could be heard from British cannons on the Harlem River and from the *Pearl*, which had edged down the Hudson to bombard American positions fifteen hundred yards north of Fort Washington. Putting ashore below Jeffrey's Hook, Washington and his lieutenants stalked toward Colonel Magaw's headquarters. The cannonade in the north had merged into an unbroken roar as the American commanders, unable to

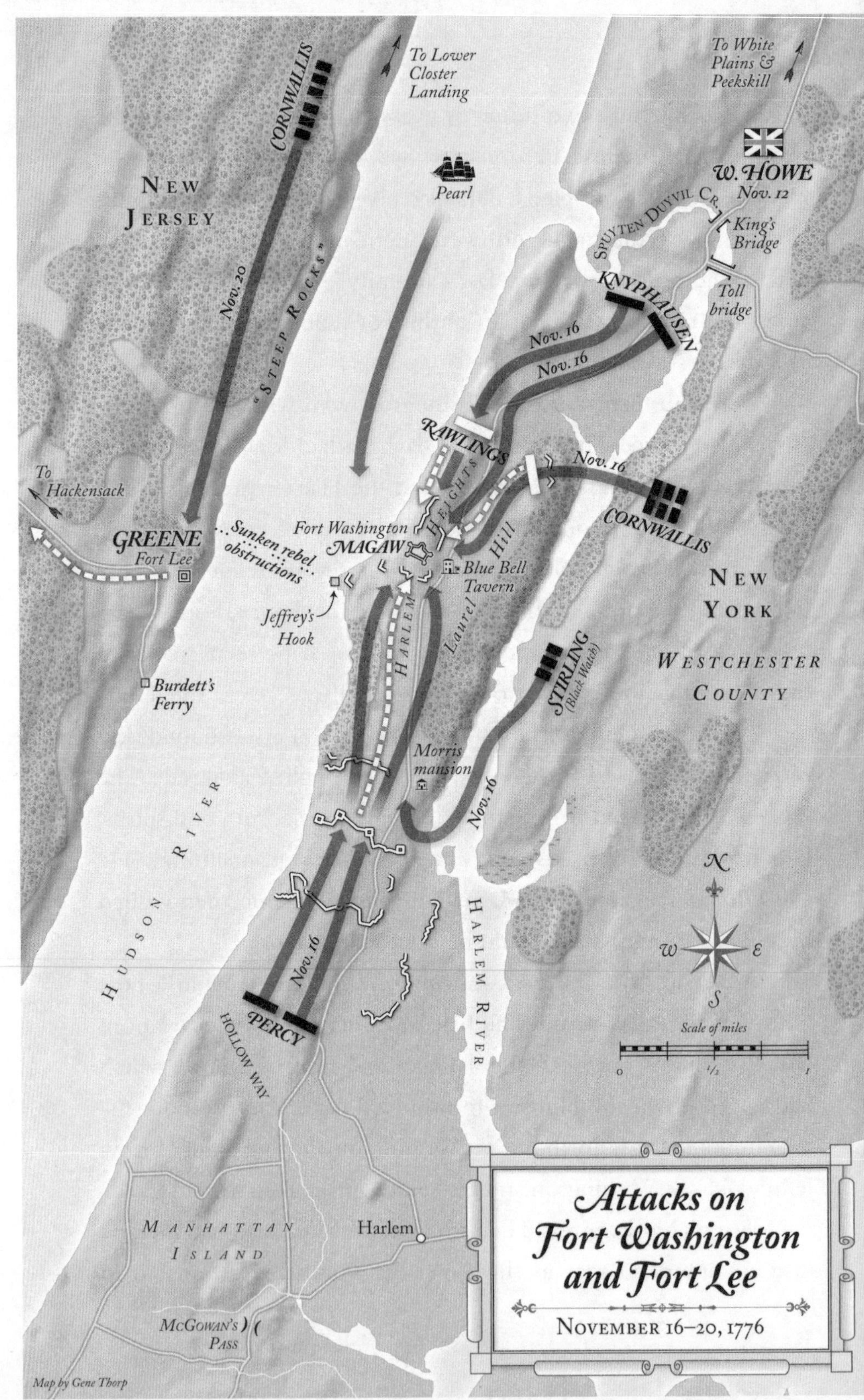

To Lower Closter Landing
To White Plains & Peekskill
CORNWALLIS
NEW JERSEY
Pearl
W. HOWE
Nov. 12
SPUYTEN DUYVIL CR.
King's Bridge
Toll bridge
KNYPHAUSEN
Nov. 20
"STEEP ROCKS"
Nov. 16
Nov. 16
RAWLINGS
HEIGHTS
Nov. 16
To Hackensack
CORNWALLIS
GREENE
Fort Lee
Sunken rebel obstructions
Fort Washington
MAGAW
Blue Bell Tavern
Hill
Laurel
NEW YORK
Jeffrey's Hook
HARLEM
WESTCHESTER COUNTY
Burdett's Ferry
STIRLING
(Black Watch)
Morris mansion
Nov. 16
HUDSON RIVER
HARLEM RIVER
N
W
E
S
Scale of miles
0
1/2
1
Nov. 16
PERCY
HOLLOW WAY
MANHATTAN ISLAND
Harlem
McGOWAN'S PASS
Map by Gene Thorp
Attacks on Fort Washington and Fort Lee
NOVEMBER 16–20, 1776

find Magaw, briefly conferred. Greene and Putnam offered to stay behind, but Washington insisted they all leave together before the enemy drew closer. Striding back to the Hudson, they climbed into the boat and returned to Fort Lee without issuing any orders and without influencing the brawl that now unfolded.

The day grew dire for Magaw's men. On the American left, General Wilhelm von Knyphausen attacked at 11:00 a.m. with more than four thousand men in two columns, which now split into three. Hessians chopped and wriggled their way through an abatis reportedly two hundred paces deep—Knyphausen himself helped yank the branches apart with his hands—then plodded across boggy ground while the *Pearl* lobbed shells and balls at rebel lines on a hillside.

The end came quickly. A courier from Fort Lee, dodging enemy bullets and bayonets as he bounded up the river bluff, brought a message from Washington urging the garrison to hold out until dark. But around 3:00 p.m., as Knyphausen paced and puffed his pipe in a stone barn barely a hundred yards from the fort, a Hessian captain walked forward with a drummer and a white flag. Magaw was soon studying another ultimatum:

> *The commander in chief demands an immediate & categorical answer to his second summons of Fort Washington. The garrison must immediately surrender prisoners of war, and give up all their arms, ammunition, & stores of every kind. The general is pleased to allow the garrison to keep possession of their baggage, and the officers to have their swords.*

Magaw asked for four hours to deliberate; he was given thirty minutes.

A few men got away. But at 4:00 p.m., nearly everyone else marched out through the breastworks toward the post road, stacking their arms between two threatening Hessian regiments. The rebels were "packed together like herring," a German chaplain wrote. "Despite the strictest orders, the prisoners received a number of blows." Men pleaded for water, for mercy, for treatment of their wounds. Dusk sifted over the fort, to be known henceforth as Fort Knyphausen and not to be repossessed by the Americans for more than seven years.

Washington had watched the disaster through his telescope from across the Hudson. He heard the pandemonium of battle, then silence, then muffled cheers as the king's colors rose over the ramparts.

Much of the Continental Army was stupefied by this latest defeat. Rumors spread that Washington would be sacked. Lee wrote on November 19, "Oh, General, why would you be overpersuaded by men of inferior judgment to your own? It was a cursed affair."

General Howe was determined to keep the Americans off-balance. At first light on November 20, with General Cornwallis in command, several dozen boats pulled across the Hudson River to Lower Closter Landing on the New Jersey shore. A rugged path—narrow, slippery, and unguarded—snaked for half a mile up to a farm lane at the rim of the bluff, 440 feet above the river. For several hours, grunting soldiers and sailors used drag ropes to haul cannons

MAJOR GENERAL LORD CHARLES CORNWALLIS. *[LOC]*

and wagons to the top. By 1:00 p.m., Cornwallis had assembled five thousand soldiers into two columns before turning toward Fort Lee, six miles south. The men moved at quick time down the rutted roads, eager to capture another American garrison.

Greene had been dozing that morning when a galloping messenger arrived with the news of redcoats seemingly levitating from the riverbank. Shrill cries rang through the fort. "Turn out! Turn out! We are all surrounded! Leave everything but your blankets!" Some men pulled on extra clothes rather than carry them in their packs, and in ten minutes the first companies headed west, then north, then west again, skirting the marshy bottomland to reach a crossroads called Liberty Pole.

Here General Washington awaited them. After being alerted by yet another galloping, wild-eyed "herald of calamity," he had dashed five miles to meet Greene and his fugitives. As Washington turned around to lead the column across the New Bridge spanning the Hackensack River, Greene rode back to Fort Lee to round up several hundred stragglers before following.

Cornwallis's legions overran the abandoned Fort Lee at dusk to find empty tents standing, kettles boiling, and skewered meat roasting by the cook fires. More than a hundred rebels were captured in the nearby woods. More booty fell into British hands, including all of the artillery, plus a thousand barrels of flour and more than two thousand head of cattle.

By Howe's reckoning, since landing at Frog's Neck six weeks earlier, his army had seized 148 guns and mortars, almost 12,000 shots and shells, and 400,000 musket cartridges. If some had once questioned Howe's determination to destroy his enemy, no one doubted that he now had the rebels on the run.

The New York campaign had ended, miserably, and New Jersey's miseries had begun. Washington and his generals had nearly lost the war several times in the past three months through miscalculation, misfortune, and deficient military skills. The Continental Army and its militia auxiliaries had been repeatedly overmatched by British regulars and their German auxiliaries.

Early Thursday morning, the little American army again assembled before trudging south. Behind them remained hundreds of dead comrades, thousands more taken prisoner, and tens of thousands of countrymen left to the mercy of an occupying army. Yet for all the misfortune of the recent weeks, for all the heartbreak and exhaustion, a flame still burned in these few as they tramped deeper into New Jersey. Stubborn and resolved, they somehow kept faith with their cause, with one another, and with generations yet unborn.

TWENTY-FOUR

FRANCE

November–December 1776

The old gentleman had gone to sea once again, despite his resolve to remain on dry land for the rest of his days. In late October, Congress had dispatched Benjamin Franklin to France in hopes of signing "a treaty with his most Christian majesty," King Louis XVI, and to obtain "twenty or thirty thousand muskets and bayonets, and a large supply of ammunition, and brass field pieces to be sent under convoy of France." The instructions tucked into his bag also empowered him to hire "a few good engineers" and to buy or borrow eight ships of the line (naval warships), "of seventy-four and sixty-four guns, well-manned." Congress had advised him it would be "proper for you to press for the immediate and explicit declaration of France in our favor," and to threaten an American reconciliation with England in the event of any French hesitation. If Franklin could persuade the French to increase their support by providing proper weapons, ships, and other military aid, the American prospects would brighten immeasurably. Rarely had a supplicant—a beggar, really—set out with greater presumption, but rarely had the court of the king seen anyone like Benjamin Franklin.

Franklin had revealed nothing publicly about his reasons for traveling. His appearance "has given birth to a thousand conjectures," one diplomat wrote. Some wondered if he had come to take the waters, or to retire to Switzerland, or to supervise the French publication of his papers. To an American ally in Paris, he wrote, "I propose to retain my incognito until I ascertain whether the court will receive ministers from the United States."

BENJAMIN FRANKLIN ARRIVES IN FRANCE IN DECEMBER 1776. [LOC]

That a large, balding American, renowned across Europe as a scientist, diplomat, and revolutionary, would remain inconspicuous as he trotted through the French provinces defied probability. Whatever the great man's purpose, Paris was alert and giddy while awaiting his arrival.

As his ship, the *Reprisal*, approached the coast of France, the headwinds kept it forty miles south of the Loire River, its intended destination. After swinging into Quiberon Bay, the ship bobbed about for four days, becalmed, to Franklin's squirming dismay. The captain hired a fishing boat to row the passengers twenty miles to Auray, a bleak and remote stone village. Franklin tottered ashore with his two grandsons, spent the night, then hired a coach for the long overland journey to Nantes.

There, the town fathers hosted a fancy dinner, a friendly

merchant replenished Franklin's purse with a loan of sixteen hundred livres, and Franklin worked on his fractured French in conversations. But after a week of waiting for *Reprisal* to arrive with his baggage, he left word to have it sent after him, bought a carriage, and, on December 15, set off for Paris, 240 miles northeast.

In the center of bustling Paris stood a slightly run-down mansion known as the Hôtel des Ambassadeurs de Hollande, even though the Dutch minister had not lived there for years. The house since late summer had swarmed with clerks, accountants, secretaries, kitchen help, and mysterious men who at all hours rapped on the great wooden door. A sign out front indicated that a Spanish financial firm occupied the premises. The firm was, in fact, the government front recently set up for shipping military supplies to America without implicating the government or embarrassing King Louis XVI. The managing director was Pierre-Augustin Caron, better known as Beaumarchais. Originally trained as a watchmaker, he had held minor court positions and made money as an arms dealer in the Seven Years' War, as a lumber merchant, and as an agent for the Crown.

In the past year, he had become an eager enthusiast for the American cause. He also believed that a victorious America could tilt the balance of power in Europe and help France avenge her catastrophic defeat in the Seven Years' War. Having lost Canada, India, and other possessions to that "usurping race"—the English—the French had been seething. He soon had a close confederate in the French foreign minister, Charles Gravier, the comte de Vergennes.

Converting the new French king to these sentiments would require artful persuasion. Though indecisive and a bit dimwitted, Louis was reasonably well disposed toward his subjects. He was also instinctively cautious in foreign affairs. Should America reconcile with Britain, Beaumarchais told the king, they might join forces to attack France. Unchecked British commercial and maritime strength would dominate Europe for generations. Aiding the Americans, on the other hand, could restore "all that the shameful peace of 1763 deprived us of" by reducing England to "a second-class power."

KING LOUIS XVI. [WIKIMEDIA COMMONS

Bit by bit the king came around, despite warnings from his finance minister that war would bankrupt France. American energy captured French imaginations and inspired young nobles, who clamored to help the insurgents against British brutality. With Louis's reluctant consent, Beaumarchais at last sprang into action with a scheme worthy of his skills. The first million livres in gold coins—equivalent to nearly £50,000—was secretly transferred from the French treasury to Beaumarchais's carriage, fairly spilling from the sacks. Spain made a similar donation six weeks later, and a third million would come from secret merchant investors in Nantes, Bordeaux, and elsewhere. Beaumarchais dashed about to Rochefort and other ports, seeking ships to charter, captains to hire, customs officials to charm or bribe. He soon accumulated surplus brass field guns and muskets from French armories and arms dealers.

Each morning, rumors circulated that Dr. Franklin had arrived in Paris, and each evening, those rumors were denied, until Saturday,

December 21, when at last the report proved true. Soon a procession of carriages brought sightseers keen to meet with "the idol of the day." Franklin received so many letters that his mail was delivered nine times a day. Some fashionable women wore wigs that imitated his fur cap, a style soon called coiffure à la Franklin. Others wore Franklin gloves, and fine eateries served chops à la Franklin. When he entered a theater, the orchestra rose in its pit and cheered.

On December 23, Franklin's grandson Temple rode ten miles to Versailles with his grandfather's written request for an audience. Five days later, at a house in Paris, the comte de Vergennes welcomed Franklin to France in a secret conference, joined by two other members of the American delegation. After mutual exchanges of flattery, Franklin explained that Congress had chosen "to make this offer first to France," which stood to benefit from the American trade that Britain had so wantonly thrown away. Vergennes stressed patience and discretion. They parted amicably, having agreed to further talks.

COUNT VERGENNES CHARLES GRAVIER, THE FRENCH FOREIGN MINISTER WHO 'GOTIATED WITH BENJAMIN FRANKLIN. [LOC]

The next evening, Franklin and his colleagues met the Spanish ambassador, the Count de Aranda, in his majestic villa on the Place Louis XV for another amiable if fruitless conversation.

On Sunday, January 5, Franklin penned another, more explicit note to Vergennes, asking for eight fully crewed warships, muskets, field artillery, and ammunition. He and his colleagues cheerfully predicted English ruination if France, Spain, and America were to make common cause. Franklin also used the only weapon he possessed: If the American war effort faltered, he warned, reconciliation with Britain seemed inevitable. America "now offers to France and Spain her amity and commerce," he concluded. "We cannot help suggesting that a considerable delay may be attended with fatal consequences." America could not defeat Britain without substantial French aid, but substantial French aid was unlikely unless America demonstrated that it could defeat Britain. His Most Christian Majesty would hardly give complete support to rebels who were not only Protestant and republican but also militarily inept. Washington and his generals must win on the battlefield.

Vergennes and his king remained skittish. A long, exquisite dance had begun. Franklin was determined to press his cause relentlessly, but with the caution the French required. Only now was he beginning to see the diplomatic complexities involved: In Europe's balance of power, France was threatened not just by Britain, but also by the ascendant Austria and Russia, and by Portuguese hostility.

Franklin quickly recognized that overbearing demands would gain little. Forbearance, persistence, persuasion, and personal charm would be needed in the coming months to align his country's interests with those of these ancient monarchies. He would listen more than speak, smile more than frown, nod more than implore.

In a dispatch to Congress, Franklin and his colleagues wrote, "The court has its reasons for postponing it a little longer. In the meantime, preparations for it are making." Still, they added in a postscript, "America should exert herself as if she had no aid to expect but from God and her own valor."

TWENTY-FIVE

NEW JERSEY

December 1776

The American army, threadbare and dying, trudged south from Newark in a pelting rain on Thursday, November 28. Muskets, discarded knapsacks, and other items littered the muddy roads. The troops numbered 5,410, but desertion thinned the ranks hour by hour. Cornwallis and his royal legions were only a few hours behind the rebels, nearly ten thousand strong in two columns moving from Newark toward Elizabeth Town and Rahway.

Among those retreating was Thomas Paine. Born in England, he had immigrated to America just two years earlier, and he had recently spent three months as a Pennsylvania militiaman before becoming General Greene's confidential assistant in mid-September. A gifted writer, his used his skill to attack slavery, dueling, animal cruelty, and the oppression of women. On January 10, 1776, a thousand copies of his new

AUTHOR AND PHILOSOPHER THOMAS PAINE. [LOC]

pamphlet on the American rebellion had been published anonymously under a simple title: *Common Sense*.

The pamphlet had sold over 150,000 copies in fifty-six editions. Paine soon revealed himself as the author, then gave up both his copyright claim and his profits, which he donated to the Continental Army for the purchase of mittens. *Common Sense* had helped nudge Americans toward their declaration of independency, converting fence straddlers into patriots and patriots into radicals. Yet the dismal events of recent months required another call for unity, a restatement of national purpose.

During the muddy trudge from Hackensack to Newark and on to New Brunswick, Paine had scribbled notes for another message, one that would be both a plainspoken meditation and a strong cry for courage. It would open with the line "These are the times that try men's souls."

Once at New Brunswick, Washington placed his headquarters in Cochrane's Tavern to avoid being outflanked and to keep his force between the British and Philadelphia, which he assumed was Cornwallis's objective.

Among other worries, Washington was uncertain where General Lee was or why he had failed to obey directions to cross the Hudson from Westchester County and rejoin the main army with his five thousand men. Greene advised Washington, "General Lee must be confined within the lines of some general plan, or else his operations will be independent of yours." In hopes of learning Lee's whereabouts, Washington opened a letter to the general's aide, Colonel Joseph Reed, while Reed was traveling on army business to Burlington. Washington instantly recognized that Lee, his senior lieutenant, and Reed, his close confidant, had conducted a

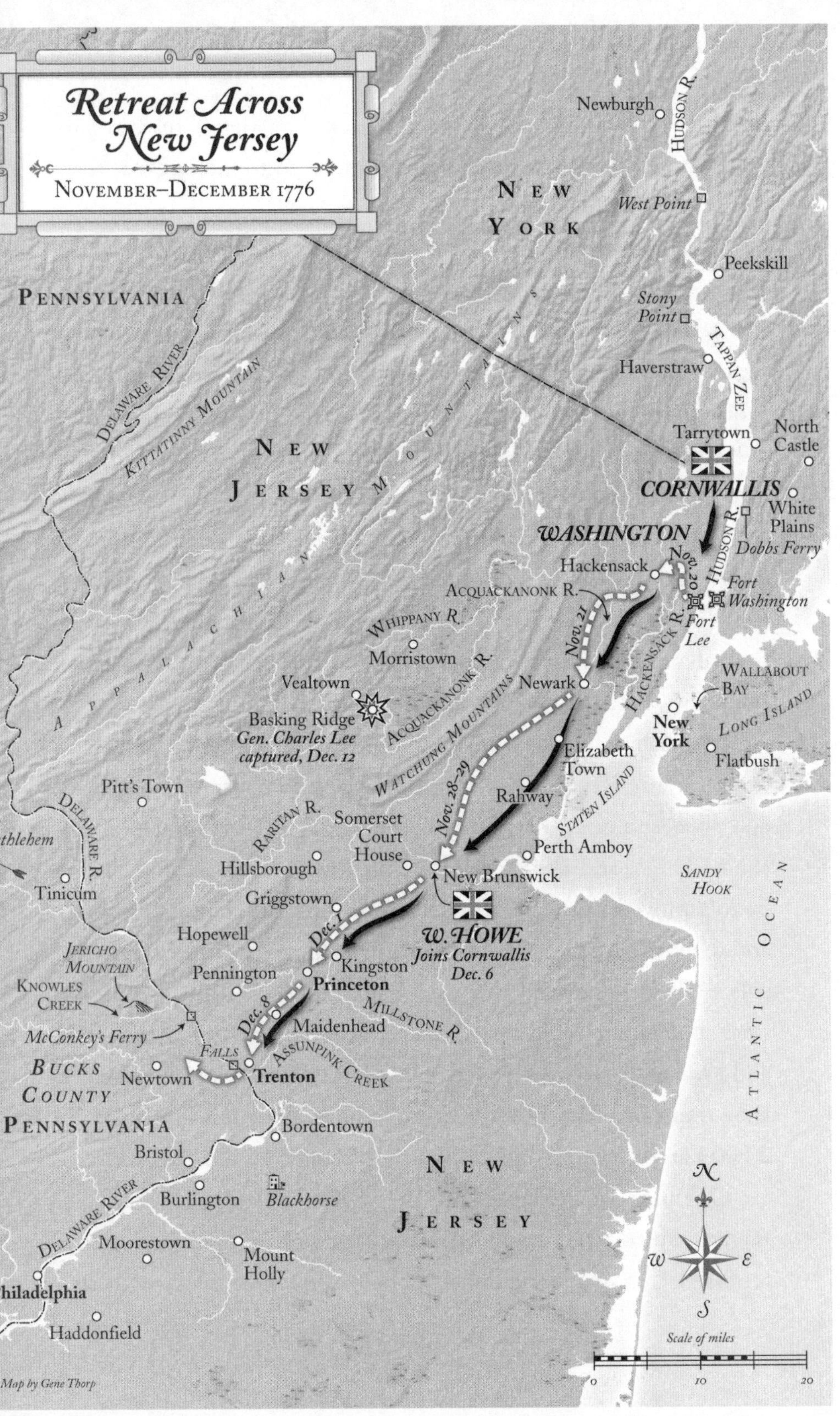

Retreat Across New Jersey
November–December 1776
New York
Newburgh
Hudson R.
West Point
Peekskill
Stony Point
Tappan Zee
Haverstraw
Tarrytown
North Castle
CORNWALLIS
White Plains
Dobbs Ferry
WASHINGTON
Hackensack
Nov. 20
Fort Washington
Fort Lee
Acquackanonk R.
Nov. 21
Whippany R.
Morristown
Newark
Wallabout Bay
Vealtown
Basking Ridge
Gen. Charles Lee captured, Dec. 12
Acquackanonk R.
Watchung Mountains
Elizabeth Town
New York
Long Island
Flatbush
Hackensack R.
Staten Island
Rahway
Nov. 28–29
Pennsylvania
Delaware River
Kittatinny Mountain
New Jersey
Appalachian Mountains
Pitt's Town
Delaware R.
ethlehem
Raritan R.
Somerset Court House
Perth Amboy
Hillsborough
New Brunswick
Sandy Hook
Tinicum
Griggstown
Hopewell
Dec. 1
W. HOWE
Joins Cornwallis Dec. 6
Jericho Mountain
Knowles Creek
Pennington
Kingston
Princeton
Millstone R.
Dec. 8
Maidenhead
McConkey's Ferry
Falls
Assunpink Creek
Bucks County
Newtown
Trenton
Pennsylvania
Bordentown
Bristol
New Jersey
Delaware River
Burlington
Blackhorse
Atlantic Ocean
Moorestown
Mount Holly
Philadelphia
Haddonfield
N
W
E
S
Scale of miles
0
10
20
Map by Gene Thorp

disloyal correspondence behind his back. Lee's letter read in part, ". . . I think yourself & some others should go to Congress & form the plan of the new army."

Washington had another serious upset just hours later when almost half of his remaining army walked away. On Sunday, December 1, the enlistments of two brigades from Maryland and New Jersey expired. Despite his personal plea to the assembled ranks, more than two thousand walked away. Most of the remaining enlistments would expire in a month. "If those go," he warned, "our force will be reduced to a mere handful."

If the army was still, by Washington's own description, "a destructive, expensive, disorderly mob," he hardly had time to fret. Scouts reported British dragoons and light infantry sweeping toward New Brunswick; Cornwallis's main legions were just two hours away, their baggage wagons stacked with loot.

So Washington kept moving. Soldiers secured two ferries on the Delaware River below Trenton. They also collected boats, oars, and poles and made rafts from scavenged boards and lumber. Every canoe, barge, and skiff for forty miles was seized or sunk. Large patrols moved upstream to guard fords and other ferry crossings, and to confiscate weapons from those hostile to the cause. The rebel galley *Warren* patrolled the west bank above Philadelphia, and a small flotilla anchored near Trenton was used to discourage spies and loyalists from crossing into New Jersey. The sick and wounded were transported to the Pennsylvania shore, along with many of the 2,000 barrels of flour and 250 bushels of salt found in Trenton.

Columns of refugees also staggered toward the Delaware River. "They called up the day of judgment," a pastor's daughter reported. "So many frightened people were assembled, with sick and wounded soldiers, all flying for their lives, and with hardly any means of crossing the river."

Puzzled by the enemy's failure to give chase, Washington started back toward central Jersey with 1,200 men led by Greene and Stirling on Saturday, December 7. The commanding general had not reached Princeton when a courier found him. The king's troops had broken camp in New Brunswick and were driving south; General Howe had arrived from New York with another brigade and now resumed his offensive with ten thousand men. Washington sent a message to recall Stirling and Greene rather than risk further combat losses. All Continental forces were to hasten for the Pennsylvania shore.

Exhausted men crowded the river. Even with stragglers arriving, the American army now numbered no more than 3,500. Boats shuttled from shore to shore, washed with light from bonfires on both banks.

Washington crossed the Delaware River shortly after dawn on Sunday morning, December 8. By noon, the rap of drums and the blare of fifes drifted across the river from Trenton, where a column

GEORGE WASHINGTON PREPARING TO CROSS THE DELAWARE IN DECEMBER 1776. [LOC]

of light infantry and three Hessian regiments strutted into town. Howe—immaculate in a gold-laced scarlet coat—soon arrived with Cornwallis at his side.

Washington put his headquarters in a brick country house half a mile from the upper Trenton ferry, ready to flee in an instant. New Jersey had been lost. Philadelphia was at risk and with it, the Congress. The British seemed unbeatable. Yet for those who had come this far and endured this much, stubborn defiance would get them through the night, and the next day, and the day following. The British, after all, had to win the war; the Americans only had to avoid losing it.

"The approach of winter putting a stop to any further progress," Howe announced, "the troops will immediately march into quarters." The fourteen thousand royalist soldiers in New Jersey built camps and hunkered down. With New York and much of New Jersey occupied, the British would find shelter and wait until spring to finish the war. Howe would return to New York for the winter and Cornwallis to England.

In Philadelphia, the approach of British troops triggered panic. Armed rebels roamed the town, closing schools and pressing teenage boys into service in militia companies. Accused loyalists were jailed. A thousand wagons were assembled to evacuate the city's riches, as well as half a million musket cartridges, public papers, and equipment from a gunlock factory. Before scurrying to safety in Baltimore, Congress ordered Philadelphia defended "to the last extremity," and Washington sent General Putnam to command the town. Putnam imposed martial law and a 10:00 p.m. curfew, effective December 12. By mid-December, at least half of Philadelphia's thirty thousand residents had fled.

✦ ✦ ✦

General Lee, at last, at long last, had indeed found his way into New Jersey. With 2,700 Continentals, joined by 1,300 militiamen, he reached Morristown on December 8, lingering there for three days in a vain hope of finding shoes and blankets for his men. He had planned to harass Howe from behind, "to unnest 'em even in the dead of winter" and force the British garrisons back to New York. But Washington would have none of it; he wanted his small army consolidated. Lee found a remote tavern in Basking Ridge for his quarters and ordered his troops to camp at Vealtown, eight miles south of Morristown. They were to prepare to swing west the next day to eventually cross the Delaware River at Tinicum, avoiding the large British force in the south before joining Washington's troops, as ordered.

Alarmed by reports that Lee was somewhere in his rear, on December 12, Cornwallis dispatched thirty-three horsemen from the 16th Light Dragoons to look for him. The riders were led by Lieutenant Colonel William Harcourt, the thirty-three-year-old son of an earl. A mile from Basking Ridge, perhaps alerted to Lee's presence by loyalist informants, Harcourt sent half a dozen scouts ahead under a young officer named Banastre Tarleton. They soon learned that Lee was in a nearby inn with little security. Colonel Harcourt quickly sketched a plan, and at 10:00 a.m., the cavalry edged through the orchard and woods around Widow White's tavern.

Inside, Lee dressed, finished his correspondence, and ordered his horse saddled for the short ride to rejoin his troops. An aide had just eaten a late breakfast when he peered from the window to see redcoats thundering down the front lane. "Here, sir, are the British cavalry!" he yelled. Tarleton clattered up to the front entrance—"making all the noise I could," he later reported—then fired into the door, bellowing, "I know General Lee is in the house!" Sixty or seventy British bullets riddled the tavern. Lee paced upstairs, dismissing a suggestion that he hide in his bed. "If the General does not surrender in five minutes," Tarleton shouted, "I will set fire to the house."

Lee stepped through the front door, bareheaded, a coat draped over his dingy white shirt. Regulars hoisted him onto a horse, tied his arms together, lashed his legs to the stirrups, and galloped south as a bugler let blare a few triumphant notes.

Upon hearing this doleful news, Washington publicly mourned the loss. But privately he voiced ambivalence about a rival who had become a thorn in his side. Later in the month, Washington wrote directly to Lee in his New York City jail cell, enclosing a draft for £116 to ease the discomfort of captivity. "I hope," he added, "you are as happy as a person under your circumstances can possibly be."

BRITISH DRAGOONS CAPTURE MAJOR GENERAL CHARLES LEE IN NEW JERSEY ON DECEMBER 12, 1776. [LOC]

In New York, Sir William Howe and his battle staff settled into their winter quarters, celebrating the apparent end of the 1776 campaign. Finally, the war seemed to be going Britain's way.

TWENTY-SIX

TRENTON, NEW JERSEY

December 24–26, 1776

For at least ten days, Washington had considered a bold lunge into the enemy's flank. "Under the smiles of Providence, we may yet effect an important stroke," he had told his lieutenants, and on this Christmas Eve they intended to review the plan for a final time. Three forces positioned along a twenty-six-mile stretch of the Delaware River would cross the river simultaneously into New Jersey before converging on Trenton with five thousand troops. The largest detachment—2,400 men with eighteen cannons—would mass under Washington's direct command on Christmas night eight miles upstream from the village. They would descend on the Hessian garrison from the north an hour before dawn on Thursday, December 26.

A shiver of excitement ran through the war council. The plan was indeed desperate, but also bold and well thought out. Together they would risk everything, following Washington wherever he led them.

Clouds thickened on Christmas Day, and the wind shifted from west to northeast. Temperatures remained below freezing. At dusk, regiments marched in columns toward the ferry crossings. Troops were reminded that upon reaching the far shore "a profound silence [is] to be enjoined & no man to quit his ranks on pain of death." It is said that no battle plan survives contact with the enemy, but this plan came unstitched even before the first gunshot. Both downstream crossings were blocked by ice piled high on the rising tide.

But beyond the reach of tidal ice, the main force under Washington nosed across the Delaware one overloaded boatload at a time. Greene's advance guard went ashore first. Back and forth the boats shuttled, several dozen troops in one freight boat and one gun or a few wild-eyed horses on the next. The hours slipped past as the winter wind howled and the temperature eased to just above freezing.

Washington waited too, eating and drinking atop his horse once he reached Jersey, his face stung with sleet. At 4:00 a.m., a command sounded through the ranks—"Shoulder your firelocks!" The column shuffled forward, stretching east from the river for more than a mile. "Press on. Press on, boys!" Washington urged, trotting along the line. Then the army divided. Greene swung left with his division, accompanied by Washington, Knox, and nine fieldpieces, to approach the town from almost due north on Scotch Road. Troops lengthened their stride in what an officer called "a long trot." The other force under General Sullivan continued onto River Road, also with nine guns, to attack from the northwest along the Delaware River.

At precisely 8:00 a.m., Lieutenant Andreas Wiederholdt listened to his soldiers' report—nothing unusual seen or heard on patrol—then stepped outside the guardhouse on Trenton's outskirts to see for himself through the freezing rain. Shadowy figures loped toward

GEORGE WASHINGTON AT THE BATTLE OF TRENTON. [LOC]

him on the road and through the bordering fields. "Der Feind! Der Feind! Heraus!" a sentry shouted. "The enemy! Turn out!" Wiederholdt heard the distant rumble of cannonading along the river to his rear. He ordered a retreat. Greene's division followed on their heels in three attack columns, heeding orders to "charge the enemy before they had time to form." Washington led in the center.

The gunfire Wiederholdt heard on River Road announced the timely arrival of Sullivan's division, led by a New Jersey company and a New Hampshire brigade commanded by Colonel John Stark. The Americans slammed into a Hessian outpost in the stable master's house behind the Hermitage, a large estate a mile upriver from Trenton. Sentries fired and fled without their knapsacks. Attackers surged through fields, gardens, and woods, and American cannoneers targeting German positions were joined by batteries shooting across the Delaware River from Pennsylvania. One American detachment headed for the old stone barracks, while a larger force pressed toward the Assunpink Bridge at the foot of Queen Street to block the enemy's retreat route to the south.

Colonel Johann Rall had passed Christmas evening playing checkers in the King Street house where he made his headquarters. The early morning clamor at both ends of Trenton failed to wake him, and only after a frantic summons from Lieutenant Jakob Piel, his adjutant, did Rall appear at a window in his nightshirt. After ducking back inside, he soon reappeared in uniform on King Street to find that the village had become a battlefield. Mounting his horse, Rall herded two of his infantry regiments behind St. Michael's Church to regroup while trying to gauge the size of the American assault. Rall tried to marshal his men. "Alle, was meine Grenadiers sein, vorwärts!" he hollered. All who are my grenadiers, forward!

But the day was lost. American soldiers flocked through the cross streets. They fired, reloaded, and fired again, deliberately targeting officers; four Hessian captains fell in short order. Two bullets knocked Rall from the saddle on the west side of Queen Street. Bleeding badly, gasping for breath, he was carried into the Methodist church and laid on a pew. Continentals demanded surrender, shouting in English and German. Finally, a battery commander told Washington, "Sir, they have struck." So they had. Hessian officers lifted their hats on sword points. Color bearers dipped their flags in submission. Jäger and grenadiers grounded their muskets or smashed them against the trees, flinging away splintered stocks and bent barrels. Some cut the straps of their cartridge pouches.

General Stirling rode forward to collect surrendered swords.

A great cheer sounded through the village, echoed in the orchard, on the bridge, and along the Assunpink. Troops tossed their

HESSIAN TROOPS SURRENDER TO GEORGE WASHINGTON AFTER THEIR DEFEAT AT TRENTON. *[LOC]*

hats in jubilation. From the initial skirmish on Pennington Road, the battle had lasted less than two hours. "Providence," Knox would write, "seemed to have smiled upon every part of this enterprise." Washington watched, no doubt with pride and perhaps amazement. As Rall's sword was collected with the other booty, the general told a subordinate, "This is a glorious day for our country."

In half a morning, Howe had lost almost a thousand of his fourteen thousand men in New Jersey. Washington's own battle casualties were minor—a dozen killed or wounded—although hundreds more still suffered from exhaustion, sickness, and cold-weather injuries, including frostbite.

Many in the Continental ranks were liberty-mad enough to favor driving Howe's legions from New Jersey, if not New York. "Never were men in higher spirits than our whole army is," a captain wrote in late December. "All are determined to extirpate them from the Jerseys." Washington was determined too, but he would move his force promptly back into Pennsylvania to regroup.

Victory at Trenton revived his reputation and enhanced his stature. Odes would be penned in his honor, with such immortal couplets as "Washington, though least expected near, / Opened fire upon the Hessians' rear." In late December, Congress granted the commanding general absolute power for six months to pay enlistment bounties, raise additional regiments, appoint all officers below the rank of general, confiscate provisions, and arrest those who refused Continental currency. Congress declared that the commander in chief "can safely be entrusted with the most unlimited power."

TWENTY-SEVEN

TRENTON, NEW JERSEY

January 1777

Heartened by his triumph on Christmas night, the commanding general decided to stay on the offensive. Several considerations led to his decision. Soon the Delaware River would freeze solid, exposing Philadelphia to attack at a time and place of General Howe's choosing. Having finally seized the initiative, Washington was loath to give it up. However, he was still uncertain how many men would join him or whether they would remain in the ranks when their enlistments expired.

After once again crossing the river to New Jersey on December 30, Washington made a plea to the regiments in Trenton. Commending their recent triumph, he spoke with urgency about winning another victory in New Jersey. He promised ten dollars for six weeks of soldiering. Yet when a drum beat for volunteers, not a man stepped forward. Washington touched the flanks of his horse with his spurs and trotted along the line, an imposing figure in his tailored blue uniform and tricorne hat. "You have done all I asked you to do, and more than could be reasonably expected," he told them, according to one sergeant's account. "But your country is at stake, your wives, your houses, and all that you hold dear." He acknowledged their "fatigues and hardships," yet stressed that "the present is emphatically the crisis which is to decide our destiny." Again the drum sounded, and this time a few men edged forward, after whispered consultations among themselves. More followed, then many more.

GEORGE WASHINGTON DEPICTED ALONG ASSUNPINK CREEK DURING THE SECOND BATTLE OF TRENTON. [LOC]

By morning, the army in Trenton would number 3,335 men fit for duty. As additional militia and Continental troops arrived, the number would double to nearly seven thousand, more than half of them Pennsylvanians.

A stiff southerly breeze brought afternoon rain on New Year's Day, turning the roads to mud said to be a "half-leg deep." The last glint of twilight had faded when Washington summoned his war council to his Queen Street headquarters. Candles flickered on the tables and sentries ringed the house as men with filthy boots and creased brows hunched over a map. Intelligence had confirmed that time was precious: A vengeful royal legion would attack within hours. No command decision would be more fateful than the one made now. Should the army retreat south, joining Colonel John Cadwalader at Crosswicks before escaping into Pennsylvania? Should the forces remain divided, with Cadwalader leading a raid on the British garrison and military stores at New Brunswick, perhaps even freeing General Lee? Or should the entire force concentrate in Trenton?

The council agreed to give battle here and now, with all forces together, Continental and militia. The commander in chief then prescribed how the brigades would deploy. A delaying force of a thousand men had already marched northeast toward Maidenhead, halfway to Princeton; they would dig in below Five Mile Run, with alarm posts farther northeast at Eight Mile Run. The main American force would hold the high ground above the Assunpink's south bank. General Knox had brought some forty field cannons across the Delaware, including the six brass pieces captured from the Hessians a few days earlier. Many of the guns would defend the bridge from Mill Hill, near the three-stone gristmill; others guarded fords up and down the creek bed. Infantry regiments would shake out for three miles in three extended lines, 250 yards apart and parallel to the Assunpink, with the left wing anchored on the Delaware River.

The urgent, high-pitched murmur of an army preparing for close combat carried on the wet night.

General Charles Cornwallis had ridden fifty hard miles from New York with dragoon outriders to arrive in Princeton late at night on January 1. He had been just hours from sailing to return home to England, his baggage already aboard *Bristol*, when a courier arrived with news of the disaster in Trenton and a request from General Howe that he take the field to put things right.

British and German staff officers soon gave Cornwallis a fair picture of his new command. Defenses had been thrown up around Princeton to prevent a surprise attack by the rebels. Since Monday, forty-two wagons had arrived with ammunition and provisions;

surplus baggage and sick troops were evacuated north. Major General James Grant, who would now be Cornwallis's deputy, had already gathered many of the finest troops in North America: guardsmen, grenadiers, Highlanders, Jäger. Of eighteen light infantry companies now in Princeton, seven had led the march to Lexington and eleven fought at Bunker Hill. For them this was a grudge match.

Drums beat to arms in Princeton well before dawn on Thursday, January 2. By first light a steady parade of regiments exited their garrisons. At noon, the army closed up sufficiently for Cornwallis to order a general advance on Trenton. American marksmen at Eight Mile and Five Mile Runs had thrown a few harassing shots before dashing back to the main skirmish line beyond Shabakunk Creek, south of Maidenhead. Here rebels demolished the bridge and concealed themselves by the hundreds in the dense forest. Riflemen led by Colonel Edward Hand lacked bayonets, but a pair of field guns anchored the ranks.

For nearly half an hour, gun batteries exchanged fire. Cannonballs sheared away tree branches and screamed down the road in both directions. Washington told Hand to "retard the march of the enemy until nightfall" if possible, then hurried back through Trenton.

Shortly before 4:00 p.m., in danger of being outflanked, Hand's rear guard whipped a few final shots across the smoke-filled hollow and fell back into the village past the King and Queen Streets junction. The running gunfight had lasted all day and kept the British column crawling at a march pace of one mile per hour.

Constant fire from behind houses and low earthworks greeted the king's men as they too poured into Trenton. To slow the enemy's

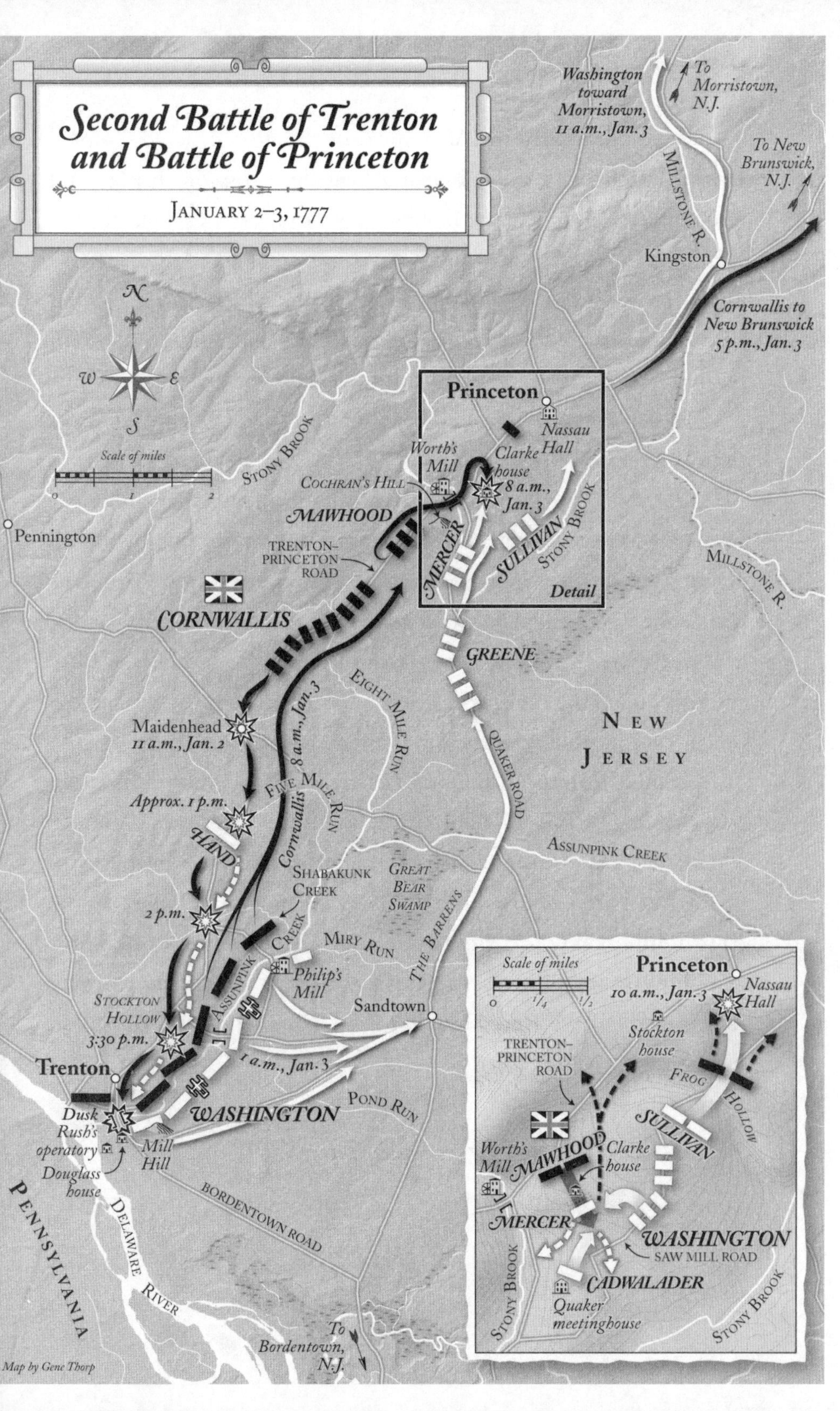

Second Battle of Trenton and Battle of Princeton
January 2–3, 1777
N
W
E
S
Scale of miles
0 1 2
Washington toward Morristown, 11 a.m., Jan. 3
To Morristown, N.J.
To New Brunswick, N.J.
Millstone R.
Kingston
Cornwallis to New Brunswick 5 p.m., Jan. 3
Princeton
Nassau Hall
Worth's Mill
Clarke house
8 a.m., Jan. 3
Cochran's Hill
Stony Brook
Mawhood
Mercer
Sullivan
Stony Brook
Detail
Pennington
Trenton–Princeton Road
Cornwallis
Millstone R.
Greene
Eight Mile Run
New Jersey
Maidenhead
11 a.m., Jan. 2
Cornwallis 8 a.m., Jan. 3
Five Mile Run
Quaker Road
Approx. 1 p.m.
Hand
Assunpink Creek
Shabakunk Creek
Great Bear Swamp
2 p.m.
Creek
Miry Run
The Barrens
Philip's Mill
Stockton Hollow
Assunpink
Sandtown
3:30 p.m.
1 a.m., Jan. 3
Trenton
Pond Run
Dusk
Rush's operatory
Washington
Mill Hill
Douglass house
Bordentown Road
Pennsylvania
Delaware River
To Bordentown, N.J.
Map by Gene Thorp
Scale of miles
0 1/4 1/2
Princeton
10 a.m., Jan. 3
Nassau Hall
Stockton house
Trenton–Princeton Road
Frog Hollow
Sullivan
Worth's Mill
Mawhood
Clarke house
Mercer
Washington
Saw Mill Road
Cadwalader
Stony Brook
Quaker meetinghouse
Stony Brook

headlong rush toward the Assunpink, Washington ordered Colonel Daniel Hitchcock's New England brigade across the bridge and into Queen Street. Muzzle flashes grew brighter as daylight faded.

From across the Assunpink, Washington ordered the men to take defensive positions in a meadow on the American left, within rifle shot of the Assunpink. Knox's gunnery had for the moment pushed enemy pursuers away from the creek, but thousands of redcoats and Hessians could be heard massing for attack in Trenton's narrow streets.

The first lunge by yowling British light infantrymen and Jäger swept toward the ford below the bridge; cannon fire from Mill Hill and a thick spray of bullets promptly turned them away. Moments later, a line of grenadiers with four field guns rushed the bridge and had crossed halfway when cannon fire from as close as forty yards pounded the ranks with frightful violence. No sooner had the defenders reloaded than the king's men charged the bridge again.

Gunners from both sides of the stream swapped fire until 7:00 p.m., aiming at muzzle flashes five hundred yards away. Washington clattered about on horseback, trailed by aides and his personal guards, to confirm that both wings were intact and alert as the day's fighting drew to a close. Exhilarated American troops kindled campfires on the hillsides, roasting skewered salt meat and cleaning their muskets. "We were ordered to rest," one sergeant scribbled in his diary.

TWENTY-EIGHT

TRENTON-PRINCETON ROAD, NEW JERSEY

January 1777

On Thursday evening, as their jaded troops bedded down in the upper village beyond the bite of Knox's guns, Cornwallis and Grant convened a war council. Cornwallis suspected that Washington intended to launch another dawn assault, like the movement against Colonel Rall's Hessians a week earlier. All regiments would be in position before sunrise, ready to smash any thrust from across the creek.

Washington in fact had backed his army across the Assunpink without a clear tactical plan for what to do next. Scouts detected an alarming concentration of assault forces on the British left. Desperate for alternatives, the commanding general convened his own war council of a dozen senior officers at General Arthur St. Clair's headquarters. As Washington listened to his lieutenants discussing their predicament, he abruptly saw with clarity a strategy as bold as crossing the Delaware River on Christmas night: The army would turn east, approaching Cornwallis's rear at Princeton before marching north toward the British logistics compound at New Brunswick. St. Clair, whose brigade of 1,400 men held the American right wing, also saw the beauty of "turning the left of the enemy in the night." So did Greene, Sullivan, Knox, Cadwalader, and others. Yes, they agreed, nodding, with glints in their eyes. Yes, this might work. They hurried off to prepare march orders and wake their men.

GEORGE WASHINGTON'S PLAN AT THE BATTLE OF PRINCETON. *[THE NATIONAL ARCHIVES]*

No man spoke above a hoarse whisper as the troops assembled. Only the generals knew their destination as more than six thousand soldiers, led by three local guides, crept from their campsites, first heading southeast away from Trenton, then east on a country lane. The column covered nine miles in six hours of freezing darkness, then halted at a road fork near a stone Quaker meetinghouse, two miles from Princeton. Here Washington divided his army as he had before attacking Trenton the previous week. Sullivan would lead the larger force of five thousand men to the right, up Saw Mill Road, falling on the village from the southern flank. Greene's smaller division of 1,500 was to head north, blocking the road to delay Cornwallis's inevitable counterattack from Trenton and Maidenhead.

American intelligence had accurately identified the size of the

British rear detachment near Princeton, but not its precise location. A midnight courier from Cornwallis had ordered two of the three regiments in Princeton to join him in Trenton, and as Washington's army crept close to the village early on Friday, more than seven hundred regulars from the 17th and the 55th Foot Regiments were marching down the road with fifty dismounted dragoons, an artillery train, supply wagons, and various convalescents and replacements. They were led by Lieutenant Colonel Charles Mawhood. The head of the British column had reached Cochran's Hill, almost two miles southwest of Princeton, when mounted British scouts reported a formation moving near the Quaker meetinghouse to the east. A dragoon lieutenant sent to investigate soon returned with alarming news: The unidentified troops were not Hessian, as Mawhood originally believed, but rebels, in long columns, marching not only toward Princeton on Saw Mill Road but also toward the road along Stony Brook. They numbered in the thousands.

The British column began to reverse its march order—no easy task on a narrow, slippery track—with the 55th Foot, originally in the rear, moving to high ground east of the road, about halfway back to the village.

The approaching force under General Greene was bound for a bridge at Worth's Mill, an obvious choke point for severing the post road. Plodding along a rutted track, the Americans could neither see nor hear the redcoats ahead. But Washington could. He concluded he was looking at a modest reconnaissance detachment heading back to Princeton, and he sent a galloper to warn Greene. He also ordered General Hugh Mercer to peel north off Saw Mill Road to intercept the enemy patrollers before they returned to the village.

Across the icy slope Mercer rode, veering to the right and keeping below the ridgeline. As he and his lead detachment emerged from a small apple orchard near the William Clarke farmhouse, the rebels suddenly confronted their enemy, barely fifty paces away. Colonel Mawhood had sent his dragoons to occupy the vacant farm. They rose as one from behind a split-rail fence and fired with a great clap and a spurt of white smoke. The Americans returned fire, targeting officers and driving the enemy back more than forty yards.

THE DEATH OF BRIGADIER GENERAL HUGH MERCER IN THE INITIAL FIGHTING AT PRINCETON, WITH GENERAL WASHINGTON IN THE BACKGROUND. [LOC]

The firing grew general. More troops, royal and rebel, charged into the fight. Scarlet stains spread in the snow. Most of Mercer's sharpshooters were riflemen whose weapons, though accurate, took much longer to reload than muskets and carried no bayonets. As the American rate of fire faltered, on Mawhood's order the British ranks charged across the farmyard with their steel bayonets extended.

The American line crumpled, then disintegrated. The American troops raced back down the icy slope in terror. Colonel Cadwalader's brigade of 1,100 men had trailed Mercer by two hundred yards, and as the battle uproar intensified ahead, the Philadelphia militia prepared to advance on Greene's order. Then Mercer's men came tearing across the fields, kicking up snow and glancing over their shoulders as they ran. A menacing crimson formation of regulars appeared behind them. Cadwalader's men edged back forty yards in confusion, briefly reformed after much noisy shoving from their officers, then broke again and bolted for the woods.

From a knoll on the American left flank, a pair of four-pounders commanded by Captain Joseph Moulder matched the British guns shot for shot and kept the redcoats from mounting another headlong assault.

The gunfire brought Washington galloping from the top of Sullivan's column, just south of Princeton. Ordering Colonel Hitchcock's New England brigade and Colonel Hand's riflemen to counterattack, he pranced among Cadwalader's militia companies, waving his hat and whooping encouragement. "Parade with us, my brave fellows," a sergeant quoted him as urging. "There is

GEORGE WASHINGTON RALLIES HIS TROOPS TO ROUT THE BRITISH AT PRINCETON. [LOC]

but a handful of the enemy, and we will have them directly." As the militia rallied—"beyond my expectation," Cadwalader admitted—Continental counterattackers surged forward, firing as they marched.

Ordered by Mawhood to "run away as fast as we could," in a British lieutenant's words, most survivors from the 17th Foot rushed up Stony Brook, then veered left for Maidenhead or plunged ahead toward Pennington. Riflemen and Philadelphia horsemen pursued the fugitives into the woodlands, urged on by Washington. Mawhood could be seen bouncing on his pony across the American front toward Princeton, his two spaniels frolicking alongside. Spotting rebel troops ahead, he wheeled west and escaped through the woods.

TWENTY-NINE

PRINCETON, NEW JERSEY

January 1777

The battle shifted into Princeton, a village with sixty houses scattered down a single street and a large stone college building, Nassau Hall, formerly revered as "a seat of learning and politeness" but now a seat of gunfire. A few troops from the 55th Foot, which had bolted from high ground off the post road, joined their 40th Foot comrades. When Sullivan's regiments pushed within musket range, the regulars fell back to a sturdy breastwork near the college yard. Some redcoats barricaded themselves inside Nassau Hall, smashing windows to shoot from the upper floors of their stone stronghold. Others simply ran for their lives.

NASSAU HALL AT THE COLLEGE OF NEW JERSEY—TODAY'S PRINCETON UNIVERSITY—WAS THE LAST BRITISH STRONGHOLD. [LOC]

The final assault included a battery of six-pounders

commanded by Captain Alexander Hamilton. The defenders who had not fled promptly surrendered. Some two hundred redcoats threw down their arms. An officer stepped from the exit with a white handkerchief on the point of his sword.

A long drum roll sounded assembly in Princeton. At 11:00 a.m., just an hour after the village had fallen, Washington gave the command and his army surged northeast, four abreast in a column on the post road. Outriders scouted for trouble, and more than two hundred prisoners shuffled with heads bowed, guarded by riflemen. A hundred cows taken from the British commissary trailed the procession. The sun had set when the army reached Somerset Court House, having covered fifteen miles in an afternoon. A thousand stragglers drifted in through the evening. Prisoners were locked up, and the troops crowded into barns or simply collapsed under wagons and in the open air.

American sentries positioned on the approach roads peered into the night in every direction and wondered what had become of their enemy.

As Washington later learned, General Cornwallis's disagreeable Friday began with the discovery at dawn that Washington's army had vanished overnight from Trenton. A suspicion that the Americans had fled south to Bordentown was dispelled by the distant sound of gunfire from Princeton. Dragoons and light infantry hurried up the road toward the village "in a most infernal sweat," as Henry Knox later wrote, "running, puffing & blowing & swearing at being so outwitted."

Cornwallis arrived at Stony Brook to find the demolished bridge sitting in the creek and a pesky pair of rebel stay-behind guns shooting at him from the far side of the gulch. After eventually pushing through the roadblock they came upon a battlefield littered with bodies, but no enemy. Nor would they be found in Princeton. The first British patrol arrived an hour after Washington's departure to discover Nassau Hall empty.

At dusk on Friday, Cornwallis led his column onto the road north from Princeton. Fearing that Washington would pillage the New Brunswick storehouses before he could get there, he abandoned some of his sick and wounded, as well as much baggage. With provisions gone, the army battered, and enemies lurking in every glade, New Jersey no longer seemed secure, much less hospitable. The fifteen-mile journey would take sixteen hours, slowed by disheartened men, spent horses, and a wrecked bridge at Kingston.

The British column stumbled into New Brunswick before first light on Saturday, January 4, to find the encampment intact and Washington reportedly headed for the secure upcountry twenty miles north, around Morristown. But Cornwallis was taking no chances: The entire garrison would be required to report with weapons to the camp perimeter long before daybreak each morning, "to be ready for the scoundrels." Every soldier was to remain armed at all times, and to listen for the three-gun signal that would summon them to their posts.

Ten thousand of the king's soldiers would spend the remainder of the winter wedged into a narrow, ten-mile strip along the Raritan, from Perth Amboy to New Brunswick, protected by the Royal Navy and surviving on salt pork. Nearly all of New Jersey had been lost. British horses and boats were positioned on Staten Island to evacuate the remaining troops if necessary.

The American army arrived at Morristown at sunset on Monday, January 6, three days after leaving Princeton. Blacksmiths repaired wagons and shoed horses, armorers fixed dilapidated firearms, and filthy, smoke-stained men washed themselves and their tattered clothes. For the first time in months, they felt secure enough to breathe deeply and sleep well.

Cornwallis assured Lord Germain on January 8 that Washington "cannot subsist long where he is." Cornwallis was wrong again; Washington was going nowhere. The army would remain in this rugged stronghold for almost five months, secure and reasonably comfortable. The Americans now had an imposing winter line that extended for 150 miles through the Hudson Highlands to Albany, from which they could harass any enemies who strayed out of New York City or New Brunswick.

Washington moved into a three-story tavern on the northwest edge of the Morristown public square. The winter campaign was over, but he hardly intended to stop fighting. Within a day, he was plotting attacks on New York. His army might rest, but he would not—could not. The cares and calamities of the past eighteen months seemed but a prelude to the worries pressing on him now, from resurgent smallpox in the ranks to the sad fact, as he wrote Hancock, that "the treasury has been for some time empty."

Certainly Washington's eighteen months in command had brought bitter lessons: that war was rarely linear, preferring a path of fits and starts, ups and downs, triumphs and disasters; that only battle could reveal those with the necessary dark heart for killing; that only those with the requisite stamina, aptitude, and luck would be able to see it through; and finally—the hardest of war's hard truths—that for a new nation to live, young men must die, often alone and in pain, and sometimes to no obvious purpose. He, more than anyone, would be responsible for ordering those men to their deaths.

For all that, he was determined to remain positive, to convey confidence and resolve. "Our affairs here are in a very prosperous train," he wrote Governor Nicholas Cooke of Rhode Island on January 20. "Within a month past, in several engagements with the enemy, we have killed, wounded, and taken prisoners between two and three thousand . . . If I am properly supported, I hope to close the campaign gloriously for America."

EPILOGUE

ENGLAND AND AMERICA

1777

As 1777 arrived, the war, of course, remained consuming to King George. He had opened the current session of Parliament by announcing that the Americans had not come to their senses, regrettably, although Canada had been recovered and success in New York offered hope for "the most decisive good consequences." He held to his theme: that the wickedness of a few American leaders was responsible for mass delusion in the colonies. "If their treason be suffered to take root," he warned, "much mischief must grow from it." He hoped that his subjects in America would reclaim "the blessings of law and liberty . . . which they have fatally and desperately exchanged for all the calamities of war and the arbitrary tyranny of their chiefs." For now, he added, "We must at all events prepare for another campaign."

Benjamin West, the gifted American artist who had lived in London for more than a decade, happened to be painting the king's portrait when a messenger brought in a copy of the Declaration of Independence. By West's account, King George grew agitated, then

***THE PAINTER BENJAMIN WEST.* [LOC]**

silent before finally muttering, "Well, if they cannot be happy under my government, I hope they may not change it for a worse."

War costs in the past two years had totaled £15 million and were increasing rapidly. The dutiful Lord North showed signs of war-weary strain. After breaking an arm in a fall from his horse, he grew seriously ill in February. Until he recovered, George would serve as his own war minister, stubborn and unmovable. In the king's library, a volume bound in red leather titled *A List of Your Majesty's Royal Navy* went on for more than a hundred pages to inform the king that he commanded 125 ships of the line—each carrying sixty guns or more—plus 270 frigates and lesser vessels, from sloops and cutters to schooners, yachts, and even hulks dating to the seventeenth century. Who could doubt the ultimate invincibility of such forces?

In late February, a request arrived from General Howe for another fifteen thousand troops and eight more warships for the spring campaign. Half of the British Army's seventy infantry regiments had already been sent to America. Even if more soldiers were dispatched, it was by no means certain that the British supply system could sustain them; feeding the force with provisions obtained

A PORTRAIT OF KING GEORGE III BY BENJAMIN WEST. [WIKIMEDIA COMMONS]

in America now appeared to be a fantasy.

The king would soldier on. The quick, decisive war he desired would not be so quick. Howe would get his men and his warships, or at least some of them. Guns, powder, and six hundred tons of tent materials had already been shipped for the battles to come.

In America, the long fighting season had finally ended, bringing to a close what John Adams would call "the most critical and dangerous period of the whole Revolutionary War." Except for the occasional raid, the battlefield would remain quiet until spring. In the two years since shots first rang out on Lexington Common, combatants had fought more than 450 military actions and 90 naval skirmishes. American casualties now approached 9,000, almost a third of them killed or wounded; of the 6,500 Americans captured, a horrific number would die in British prisons.

The American army had not been skilled in any conventional sense. Yet an American way of war was emerging, one that stressed hit-and-run actions, good marksmanship, quick recovery, and support from the people; as Washington intended, the army could claim deep emotional and moral ties to the nation it served. The integration of state militias into a national, professional armed force would remain a perpetual struggle. Despite Washington's incessant grumbling about militia indiscipline, the local companies had proven to be essential in suppressing loyalists, confronting enemy scavengers, gathering intelligence, protecting civilians, and providing combat reserves at crucial moments.

Holding together the army and, thus, the cause would inevitably fall to Washington. He listened to advice, learned from mistakes, and showed a keen eye for judging talent. As a political general, he would have few equals and no superior in American history; he had skillfully won over both the Congress and his countrymen. Since his appointment to lead the new army, Washington had developed a shrewd understanding of the stubborn, independent peoples known collectively as Americans. "A people unused to restraint must be led," he wrote in January 1777; "they will not be drove." He was a leader.

The cause was hardly won. Independence had been proclaimed, not secured. The bloodletting had just begun. Faith would be needed to sustain these revolutionaries—faith in one another and in the America they imagined could emerge from this conflict.

FORMING AN AMERICAN ARMY

As the arguments with Great Britain escalated through the 1760s and early 1770s, the colonies of course had armed troops. Many towns or villages had formed militias, a group of armed men who guarded against American Indians or other attackers. Some British troops also were based in New England and on the colonial frontier to keep the peace.

When George Washington was named to command the new Continental Army in June 1775, he had to organize the militias into an army. Among his many responsibilities, he supervised countless military tasks, from getting food for his troops to obtaining cannons and ammunition. An army needed messengers, horses, maps, boats for crossing rivers, spies, tents, wagons, uniforms, and many other things. Soldiers needed training in how to move quickly, shoot accurately, and obey orders. These tasks would occupy Washington and his officers for many months.

In exchange for a small salary, American soldiers agreed to serve in the ranks for a fixed period of time, which at the beginning of the Revolution was often as brief as a few months or a year. When their stint was finished, they could and often did simply walk away despite pleas from their officers to reenlist.

BRITISH TROOPS AND MERCENARIES

By the middle of 1776, there were more than thirty thousand British soldiers in the colonies. They had been sent to fight the rebellious colonists and to force Americans to remain subjects of the British empire. Many British officers were the younger sons of wealthy families, while common soldiers typically came from the lower social classes and often made the army a profession for life. Among the best troops in the British army were men from the Scottish Highlands.

To further strengthen the fighting force in America, the British government also hired thousands of German mercenary soldiers. They were known as Hessians after the region of Germany where most of them lived. In addition to land forces, Britain had the greatest navy the world had ever seen. Dozens of Royal Navy warships would sail into American waters.

DECLARATION OF INDEPENDENCE

IN CONGRESS, July 4, 1776.

The unanimous Declaration of the thirteen united States of America,

When in the Course of human events, it becomes necessary for one people to dissolve the political bands which have connected them with another, and to assume among the powers of the earth, the separate and equal station to which the Laws of Nature and of Nature's God entitle them, a decent respect to the opinions of mankind requires that they should declare the causes which impel them to the separation.

We hold these truths to be self-evident, that all men are created equal, that they are endowed by their Creator with certain unalienable Rights, that among these are Life, Liberty and the pursuit of Happiness.–That to secure these rights, Governments are instituted among Men, deriving their just powers from the consent of the governed, –That whenever any Form of Government becomes destructive of these ends, it is the Right of the People to alter or to abolish it, and to institute new Government, laying its foundation on such principles and organizing its powers in such form, as to them shall seem most likely to effect their Safety and Happiness. Prudence, indeed, will dictate that Governments long established should not be changed for light and transient causes; and accordingly all experience hath shewn, that mankind are more disposed to suffer, while evils are sufferable, than to right themselves by abolishing the forms to which they are accustomed. But when a long train of abuses and usurpations, pursuing invariably the same Object evinces a design to reduce them under absolute Despotism, it is their right, it is their duty, to throw off such Government, and to provide new Guards for their future security.–Such has been the patient sufferance of these Colonies; and such is now the necessity which constrains them to alter their former Systems of Government. The history of the present King of Great Britain is a history of repeated injuries and usurpations, all having in direct object the establishment of an absolute Tyranny over these States. To prove this, let Facts be submitted to a candid world.

He has refused his Assent to Laws, the most wholesome and necessary for the public good.

He has forbidden his Governors to pass Laws of immediate and pressing importance, unless suspended in their operation till his Assent should be obtained; and when so suspended, he has utterly neglected to attend to them.

He has refused to pass other Laws for the accommodation of large districts of people, unless those people would relinquish the right of Representation in the Legislature, a right inestimable to them and formidable to tyrants only.

He has called together legislative bodies at places unusual, uncomfortable, and distant from the depository of their public Records, for the sole purpose of fatiguing them into compliance with his measures.

He has dissolved Representative Houses repeatedly, for opposing with manly firmness his invasions on the rights of the people.

He has refused for a long time, after such dissolutions, to cause others to be elected; whereby the Legislative powers, incapable of Annihilation, have returned to the People at large for their exercise; the State remaining in the mean time exposed to all the dangers of invasion from without, and convulsions within.

He has endeavoured to prevent the population of these States; for that purpose obstructing the Laws for Naturalization of Foreigners; refusing to pass others to encourage their migrations hither, and raising the conditions of new Appropriations of Lands.

He has obstructed the Administration of Justice, by refusing his Assent to Laws for establishing Judiciary powers.

He has made Judges dependent on his Will alone, for the tenure of their offices, and the amount and payment of their salaries.

He has erected a multitude of New Offices, and sent hither swarms of Officers to harrass our people, and eat out their substance.

He has kept among us, in times of peace, Standing Armies without the Consent of our legislatures.

He has affected to render the Military independent of and superior to the Civil power.

He has combined with others to subject us to a jurisdiction foreign to our constitution, and unacknowledged by our laws; giving his Assent to their Acts of pretended Legislation:

For Quartering large bodies of armed troops among us:

For protecting them, by a mock Trial, from punishment for any Murders which they should commit on the Inhabitants of these States:

For cutting off our Trade with all parts of the world:

For imposing Taxes on us without our Consent:

For depriving us in many cases, of the benefits of Trial by Jury:

For transporting us beyond Seas to be tried for pretended offences

For abolishing the free System of English Laws in a neighbouring Province, establishing therein an Arbitrary government, and enlarging its Boundaries so as to render it at once an example and fit instrument for introducing the same absolute rule into these Colonies:

For taking away our Charters, abolishing our most valuable Laws, and altering fundamentally the Forms of our Governments:

For suspending our own Legislatures, and declaring themselves invested with power to legislate for us in all cases whatsoever.

He has abdicated Government here, by declaring us out of his Protection and waging War against us.

He has plundered our seas, ravaged our Coasts, burnt our towns, and destroyed the lives of our people.

He is at this time transporting large Armies of foreign Mercenaries to compleat the works of death, desolation and tyranny, already begun with circumstances of Cruelty & perfidy scarcely paralleled in the most barbarous ages, and totally unworthy the Head of a civilized nation.

He has constrained our fellow Citizens taken Captive on the high Seas to bear Arms against their Country, to become the executioners of their friends and Brethren, or to fall themselves by their Hands.

He has excited domestic insurrections amongst us, and has endeavoured to bring on the inhabitants of our frontiers, the merciless Indian Savages, whose known rule of warfare, is an undistinguished destruction of all ages, sexes and conditions.

In every stage of these Oppressions We have Petitioned for Redress in the most humble terms: Our repeated Petitions have been answered only by repeated injury. A Prince whose character is thus marked by every act which may define a Tyrant, is unfit to be the ruler of a free people.

Nor have We been wanting in attentions to our Brittish brethren. We have warned them from time to time of attempts by their legislature to extend an unwarrantable jurisdiction over us. We have reminded them of the circumstances of our emigration and settlement here. We have appealed to their native justice and magnanimity, and we have conjured them by the ties of our common kindred to disavow these usurpations, which, would inevitably interrupt our connections and correspondence. They too have been deaf to the voice of justice and of consanguinity. We must, therefore, acquiesce in the necessity, which denounces our Separation, and hold them, as we hold the rest of mankind, Enemies in War, in Peace Friends.

We, therefore, the Representatives of the united States of America, in General Congress, Assembled, appealing to the Supreme Judge of the world for the rectitude of our intentions, do, in the Name, and by Authority of the good People of these Colonies, solemnly publish and declare, That these United Colonies are, and of Right ought to be Free and Independent States; that they are Absolved from all Allegiance to the British Crown, and that all political connection between them and the State of Great Britain, is and ought to be totally dissolved; and that as Free and Independent States, they have full Power to levy War, conclude Peace, contract Alliances, establish Commerce, and to do all other Acts and Things which Independent States may of right do. And for the support of this Declaration, with a firm reliance on the protection of divine Providence, we mutually pledge to each other our Lives, our Fortunes and our sacred Honor.

[The 56 signatures on the Declaration appear in the positions indicated:]

GEORGIA

Button Gwinnett, Lyman Hall, George Walton

NORTH CAROLINA

William Hooper, Joseph Hewes, John Penn

SOUTH CAROLINA

Edward Rutledge, Thomas Heyward, Jr., Thomas Lynch, Jr., Arthur Middleton

MASSACHUSETTS

John Hancock

MARYLAND

Samuel Chase, William Paca, Thomas Stone, Charles Carroll of Carrollton

VIRGINIA

George Wythe, Richard Henry Lee, Thomas Jefferson, Benjamin Harrison, Thomas Nelson, Jr., Francis Lightfoot Lee, Carter Braxton

PENNSYLVANIA

Robert Morris, Benjamin Rush, Benjamin Franklin, John Morton, George Clymer, James Smith, George Taylor, James Wilson, George Ross

DELAWARE

Caesar Rodney, George Read, Thomas McKean

NEW YORK

William Floyd, Philip Livingston, Francis Lewis, Lewis Morris

NEW JERSEY

Richard Stockton, John Witherspoon, Francis Hopkinson, John Hart, Abraham Clark

NEW HAMPSHIRE

Josiah Bartlett, William Whipple

MASSACHUSETTS

Samuel Adams, John Adams, Robert Treat Paine, Elbridge Gerry

RHODE ISLAND

Stephen Hopkins, William Ellery

CONNECTICUT

Roger Sherman, Samuel Huntington, William Williams, Oliver Wolcott

NEW HAMPSHIRE

Matthew Thornton

GLOSSARY OF 18TH CENTURY MILITARY TERMS

ABATIS: a pile of cut trees with their sharpened branches facing toward the enemy to prevent surprise and delay an attacking enemy once within the defenders' range

BASTION: a part of a fortification projecting outward to allow defensive fire in several directions

BATEAU (pl. bateaux): a light, flat-bottomed boat used on rivers

BATTERY: a group of artillery pieces such as the guns on a warship; also a fortified structure for guns

BREASTWORK: a temporary fortification made of piled material (logs, fence rails, stones) usually built up to breast height

BROADSIDE: the simultaneous discharge of all guns on one side of a ship

DRAGOON: a member of a European military group on horseback

DRUB: to defeat soundly

ENTRENCHMENT: a long cut (trench) dug into the earth with the dirt piled up into a mound in front to shelter inhabitants from enemy fire and delay an enemy's approach

FIRELOCK: a gun that uses a spark to ignite the powder charge

FLANK: the right or left side of a group of soldiers

FLANKER: a fortification threatening the side of a force

FLINT: material used for producing a spark

FRIGATE: a sailing warship

FRONT: the area where the front lines in a conflict are engaged in fighting

FUSILIER: a soldier armed with a flintlock musket

GAITER: a cloth or leather lower-leg covering

GALLEY: a long, low ship propelled by oars; used for warfare, piracy, and trading

GARRISON: a building occupied by troops stationed in a town to defend it; also the troops stationed there

GRAPESHOT: ammunition consisting of a cluster of small iron balls fired from a cannon

GRENADIER: a category of soldiers, often considered particularly large or strong, who had once thrown exploding grenades in battle

KIT: a set of articles forming part of a soldier's equipment

LIBERTY POLE: a tall mast with a flag or other article symbolizing liberty at its top

LIGHT COMPANIES: soldiers with lighter-weight equipment and arms, making them more mobile

MORTAR: a cannon with a short muzzle positioned to fire high above walls

OUTFLANK: to get around an opposing force

RAMPART: a broad earthen mound surrounding a fortified place to protect it from artillery fire and infantry assault

RAMROD: a rod for ramming home the charge in a muzzle-loaded firearm

REDOUBT: an enclosed fortification constructed to defend a position from attack from any direction

SIEGE: a military strategy with the objective of blocking the supply lines and escape routes of a city or encampment in order to force its surrender

SKIFF: a small, flat-bottomed rowboat

SPIKE (a gun): to disable a gun by driving a spike into the vent

STRIKE: to lower a flag or sail to signal surrender

THEATER: the entire area where armed conflict is taking place

TOPMAST: the mast directly above the lowest mast

TRANSPORT (ship): a ship for carrying soldiers and military equipment

VANGUARD: troops moving at the head of a military unit

VOLLEY: simultaneous discharge of weapons

GLOSSARY SOURCES

American Battlefield Trust, "A Glossary of Fortification Terms," battlefields.org/learn/articles/glossary-fortification-terms

Lexico, lexico.com

Merriam-Webster's Collegiate Dictionary, 11th Edition

SOURCE NOTES

Atkinson, Rick. *The British Are Coming: The War for America, Lexington to Princeton, 1775–1777*. New York: Henry Holt and Company, 2019.

Sebree, Chet'la and Susan Provost Beller. *Historical Sources on the Revolutionary War*. New York: Cavendish Square, 2020.

Schmittroth, Linda. *American Revolution: Biographies*. Detroit: UXL/Gale, 2000.

MAKING THE AMERICAN REVOLUTION COME TO LIFE

Visit www.revolutiontrilogy.com or https://www.mountvernon.org/library/author-interviews/rick-atkinson/ to watch videos by the author interwoven with wonderful archival photographs on the topics:

George Washington: A Novice General

King George III and the American Revolution

The Siege of Boston, 1775

George Washington's Defeat in New York

The Crucial Revolutionary Battles of Princeton and Trenton

PLACES TO VISIT

MINUTEMEN MONUMENT, LEXINGTON, MA
HTTPS://CATALOG.ARCHIVES.GOV/ID/135803240

MONUMENT TO THE MEN OF THE REVOLUTIONARY WAR, CONCORD, MA
HTTPS://CATALOG.ARCHIVES.GOV/ID/135803224

GRAVE OF FIRST BRITISH SOLDIERS KILLED AT CONCORD, MA
HTTPS://CATALOG.ARCHIVES.GOV/ID/135803244

MONUMENT TO WILLIAM PRESCOTT AT BUNKER HIL

INDEX